Oysters
&
Champagne

Oysters & Champagne

Choice Morsels from *Wheeler's Review*

Edited by
PAT DAVIS

ROBERT HALE · LONDON

First published in Great Britain in 1986

Robert Hale Limited
Clerkenwell House
Clerkenwell Green
London EC1R 0HT

British Library Cataloguing in Publication Data

Oysters and champagne : choice morsels from
Wheeler's Review.
1. Food   2. Beverages
I. Davis, Pat   II. Wheeler's Review
641   TX353

ISBN 0-7090-2792-3

To my wife, without whose unstinting help this repast – and so many
others – would never have reached the table

Design by Catrina Restall

Photoset in North Wales by
Derek Doyle & Associates, Mold, Clwyd.
Printed in Great Britain by
St Edmundsbury Press Ltd, Bury St Edmunds, Suffolk.
Bound by WBC Bookbinders Ltd.

Contents

Soup

Fish

Sorbet

Contents

A Toast!

Coffee and Liqueurs

Cigars

Envoi

Foreword

by Auberon Waugh

Reading through these pages, I decided it was a kind and thoughtful thing of the Reverend Simon Phipps, in offering a Grace Before Meat, to remind us of the world's starving. In a book which was otherwise dedicated to the celebration of good wine and good food, there was something missing – something which it has been the function of clergymen, through the ages, to provide. Like a sorbet between two gigantic main courses, Grace before the beginning of a large meal sharpens the appetite, and elevates the whole proceedings from an image of pigs at the trough to something approaching a ritual.

Perhaps the Foreword to a collection of writings on food and wine has a similar role. If wine is hard to write about without sounding silly, food is almost impossible to describe without making readers feel slightly sick. A few can do it, but many fail. There is always a temptation to gloat, and although one can usually get away with gloating about wine, especially if there is a nostalgic element in the gloating – wines we drank then which we will never drink again – food remains tricky, even after many years.

Reading novels of the fifties and sixties, I am often puzzled by the way that whenever the characters drink claret, they always drink Château Lafite; whenever they drink Burgundy, it is always La Tache. How many undergraduates today could possibly afford to serve La Tache at a luncheon party for twelve, as Gilbert Harding says he did at Cambridge? Very few serious wine drinkers in England will nowadays taste either wine from one year's end to the next. Yet the wines are still there to be drunk in happier lands, where people work harder than we do and there is more money to spend on the things which make one proud to be human.

But whatever may have happened to the English, we still have the best oysters in the world. Even if we can no longer afford to drink the best wines of Burgundy and Bordeaux, we can still afford to drink champagne – in fact we drink more and more of it with every year that passes. Although it is possible to pay enormous sums for the prestige cuvées, the authorities in Rheims and Epernay see to it that there is virtually no such thing as a bad bottle of champagne.

Life goes on, and in many respects seems to improve. Miss Nancy Spain writes on page 225 that 'good journalists seldom eat', as if it was a rule of life. What an epitaph for a brave woman! The journalists I know seem to do little else. *Oysters and Champagne* confirms my belief that the only way to celebrate eating and drinking is to recall the joy these activities bring to us, and will continue to bring so long as the puritans and social reformers are kept at bay. Absurd we may be, we browsers and sluicers, but our pleasures are extraordinarily harmless beside those of the politicians and power-seekers.

A.W.

Editor's Preface

Antony Wysard, a Harrovian of rugged Norman-Scots line, youthfully spurned the dry figures of accountancy for the live ones of self-taught line-and-wash caricatures. The Society glossies, *Tatler*, *Sphere* and *Bystander*, clamoured for them. He also executed a series of line drawings for the *Sunday* and the *Daily Express*. In 1936 his one-man exhibition (which included caricatures depicting as many as ninety well-known personalities) was widely acclaimed by the critics.

Somehow he found time to act also as personal assistant to an MP, and as director of advertising to Alexander Korda's film studios at Denham.

Foreseeing the war, he became commissioned in the Queen's Westminster (TA) in 1938, but it was with the Green Jackets that he served throughout the war. In the Middle East he helped to raise a phantom army to haunt the German High Command!

Demobbed, with typical flair he became associate editor of *Harper's Bazaar* and set up his own advertising consultancy. This was the launch-pad in 1955 for *Wheeler's Review*. It was a subtle brainwave, the softest of cultured soft sells, that was to turn advertising into art and to be eagerly welcomed in over 100 countries during twenty-nine years.

His name is also closely associated with the founding of the famous Thursday Club, for which he and other talented writers and artists foregathered at the Old Compton Street bar. Proprietor Bernard Walsh, who revelled in wise and witty talk and high spirited camaraderie, set aside an upper room there in which to wine and later dine them. From them, Wysard chose an incomparable team that offered a blend of wit and intellect as smooth as vintage port.

* * *

The first issue of *Wheeler's Review* swept in on the breath of 1955's spring. For variety and savour the menu vied with Wheeler's own. Old Compton, as maître d'hôtel, ushered it in with an astrological conjunction of food and wine; John Pudney versified the oyster's 'perfect breeding'; James Laver (not yet Sir) made a sartorial survey of the 'Waiter!' through the ages; Gilbert Harding untetchily remembered a Cambridge college luncheon; Patrick Campbell poured out a vitriolic 'Hymn of Hate' against those 'who play the goat with cigars'; Bruce Blunt rustled the first of his long succession of 'Vine

11

Leaves' as he tasted 'Some Wines of 1954'; Ursula Bloom killed Sabbatarian *ennui* with 'Sunday in London'; and Bernard Walsh gave the 'off' to his 'Focus on Racing'. It was all as amusing, intimate, wide ranging and stimulating as the best after-dinner conversation.

What a cast! And one with backcloths ranging from crisp Wysard caricatures to striking Baron and John Gay photographs, and with other illustrations running the gamut from Rowlandson and Beardsley to Hogarth and the Luttrell Psalter. The company was picked, the stage chosen, and equally talented understudies were waiting in the wings: Epicurus, Vernon Jarratt, Sir John Betjeman, D.B. Wyndham Lewis, Simon Harcourt-Smith, Spike Hughes, Hector Bolitho, Macdonald Hastings....

After twenty-six years, illness forced Antony Wysard to retire. Slightly apprehensive but delighted, in 1981 I was offered the daunting task of following in his footsteps. From then until 1984 my delight in *WR*, its previous editor and contributors and a new team of equally outstanding writers, continued to grow.

It is to honour them, Antony Wysard and the *Review* itself that this anthology has been joyously compiled. It deals only with Wheeler's *raison d'être*; perhaps one day the remaining brilliant articles may well be another story....

And it is to *all* contributors, both Antony Wysard's and my own, that I gratefully extend my warmest thanks not merely for so readily giving me permission to use their articles but also for their enthusiastic support. I am sure that *Oysters and Champagne* has savour and sparkle enough to keep *Wheeler's Review*'s memory evergreen. How richly it deserved it!

I am perhaps even more indebted to Mrs Antony Wysard for her generous permission to reproduce a number of her late husband's brilliant caricatures and illustrations. Without them the essential *Review* charisma would have been lacking.

My thanks are also due to Micael Golder, Chairman of Wheeler's Restaurants for his ready permission to reproduce from *Wheelers Review*.

Strenuous endeavour has been made to contact all contributors. But with a thirty-year time span this has not been possible in every case. The Editor feels sure these few would have been as generously helpful as the many and hopes, if they see their words in print, that they will write to him.

Grace

Grace Before Meat

The Rev Simon Phipps

Chaplain of Trinity College, Cambridge (Now Bishop of Lincoln)

Religion and the Ridiculous are subtly related. It is only of recent years that clergymen have been treated as serious characters on the stage, curates less often vying now with mothers-in-law as sure game for an easy laugh. Perhaps the link that connects these two profound factors in human life is a sense of proportion.

Things normal are things in their right proportion, properly balanced, and excite no merriment. It is the abnormal, even the ever so faintly abnormal, that amuses. It literally tickles our fancy, stimulating and evoking a whole impossible world of imagination. It is said, for instance, that Charles II quite dissolved to see Nell Gwynn in an abnormally large hat.

Distinction of proportion may, however, be more subtle than this, and nowhere more so than in the realm of religion. A Christian certainly believes that ultimately the only right proportion in which things may be seen is that set by the schemes of Christian belief. To him the only true relationship of nature, man and God is that implied by Christianity.

Perhaps, therefore, it is the particular ultimacy of this proportion, covering as it does the whole of this life and, as far as we can 'see', of the next, that makes any disturbance of its balance so particularly ridiculous. Nowhere is a fit of the giggles more agonisingly unsuitable nor more irresistibly infectious than in a church. The smallest change in emphasis in a reading of scripture, the least shift of balance and proportion, may let loose a gale of hilarity to the helpless discomfort of those concerned.

'And they did eat.' With these reasonable words the story of the feeding miracle concludes. 'And they *did* eat.' The whole thing, thus changed, transports us willy-nilly into the ridiculous realm of incredulous nannies discussing a children's party.

The subject of Grace before Meat provides ample examples of these fine distinctions, the more so since it is a wholly reasonable practice in itself. Nowadays it is all too readily relegated to the nursery – or perhaps we should say, since the nursery is a vanishing sphere, to childhood. Grown-ups don't say grace. It is left behind with the sailor suit, the milk of magnesia and the pomade divine.

Yet in a world bearing the miserable and shameful burden of 40,000,000 refugees, in a world half of whose population is under-nourished, the custom of saying grace seems reasonable and 'grown-up' enough. The refugees in Jordan – 850,000 of them – are fed by UNO, but they get neither meat nor fresh vegetables in their meagre diet.

But with this said, remembered and practically responded to with generosity, there *is* a lighter side. How often does grace lend itself to humour when things go slightly awry! So rare, comparatively, is the custom today that we parsons often find ourselves in a dilemma: shall we be asked to say grace, or no? Do we, while the others sit down, hang about expectantly behind a chair and wait with increasing huffiness to be asked to perform? Or do we slide merrily into our seat, to find everyone standing in cold and disapproving anticipation? Are we to be thought prigs or *roués*? The first situation may be carried off with a sort of jolly 'Oh, well ...' smile all round, as one catches up on the first dish. There is, however, little to dispel the silent, watched indignity of the second as one lamely rises, and how hollow and accusing one's words sound thereafter! It was no human parson who implicitly accused an over-eager fellow-diner with the grace: 'For what we are about to receive, and for what Mr Thompson has already received, may the Lord make us truly thankful.'

It is, of course, possible to be overaccustomed to grace, as was the case of a small girl who, about to meet Archbishop Temple and being warned not to forget to say 'Your Grace' to the Archbishop, approached the ample figure with: 'For what we are about to receive ...'.

But childhood passes and soon the prison-house shades of school close upon the growing boy. The popular conception of life at a public school still inclines to one of unstinted luxury and soft little Tory boys;

in fact the rigours of its discipline and scant comfort would surprise the uninitiated. Particularly the food! The lamentable culinary standard is part of the system, breeding those qualities of endurance and sang-froid that make for leadership in Englishmen. Many a war has been won for us in the dining-rooms of Eton. I recall my own housemaster's reply to my father's letter complaining on my behalf about the food.

'The food', he wrote, 'is not markedly unappetizing.' Gently he was pointing out the follies of luxury. A reasonable dollop of cornflower shape – like the winter climate of the Thames Valley and bathing in the accumulated sewage of Maidenhead and Marlow – was *good* for a boy. Yet even this standard had its zero, and once, when a boys' dinner sank to a new low, a housemaster was heard to intone, 'For what we have received may the Lord make us sufficiently content.'

Scholars in college at Eton are called to grace in their hall at the end of a meal with the injunction: 'Surgite!' – Arise! – shouted by the captain of the school. When the Provost was dining at the high table, by careful timing the command would be shouted just as the great man had filled his mouth with biscuit and cheese. His embarrassment was complete. Was he to munch brazenly through the Latin grace that followed, accompanying it with the rhythmic sounds of a slightly cracked gramophone record, or should he stand there scarletly stuffed with Stilton and cream crackers?

This predicament evokes the memory of another, reported at the time in the Press. After a garden party at Buckingham Palace, apparently, there was discovered behind a shrub in the palace grounds a pair of false teeth embedded in a meringue. Exactly what panic-stricken grace was offered up for that royal repast must for ever remain a fascinating speculation. At least it will not have been conventional, and there is a certain freshness about all unconventional, extempore prayers which come from the heart. Such was the conviction of the minister who, in 'asking a blessing' before meat, would say: 'For baked eggs in cream, *and* roast lamb *and* mint sauce, and *potatoes* ... er, boiled potatoes? ... yes, *boiled* potatoes and *peas*' – in a mouth-watering crescendo as he lifted cover after cover – 'thank God.'

What fun he must have had, not unlike the parson who, having lost a page in his prayer book from the Benedicite, extemporised with anything that occurred to him in pairs:

O ye Bread and Butter, bless ye the Lord:
O ye Whisky and Soda, bless ye the Lord:
O ye Marshall and Snelgrove, bless ye the Lord:
Praise Him and magnify Him for ever.

We hear, too, of Bishop Wilberforce's acquaintance who would first look to see if champagne glasses were set on the table for dinner, and if so, would begin: 'O most bountiful Jehovah! ...'

If, however, there were only claret glasses to be seen, he would intone: 'We are not worthy, O Lord, of these, the least of Thy mercies ...'

Latin graces only lend themselves to the extremes of donnish humour or schoolboy howler, such as, 'Benito benedictator' or 'Benedictine benedecantor'.

Let me end, as most children's graces end: 'Amen-please-may-I-get-down?'

Winter 1956

Waiter!

Waiter!

A Brief Social and Sartorial Survey

James Laver

Waiter! Garçon! Herr Ober! Cameriere! The word, and the man, is familiar in all the civilised nations of the world. And his extension is not only in space, but in time. So soon as man emerges from barbarism the waiter appears. He has been on his feet ever since, and when he disappears we can be sure that a new barbarism is approaching; a world in which everybody will draw standardised food from a canteen-hatch. *Vive le garçon!* Long live the waiter!

What is the history of so persistent and useful a member of the community? In wall-paintings, papyri and stone-carvings we can trace him back a long way. We find him in Ancient Egyptian records, although the Pharaohs seem to have had a preference for waitresses – singularly unclad. Such waiters as there were wore the skirt or loincloth worn by all but the highest ranks of society. The black coat and boiled shirt was still far into the future. The Greeks and Romans had serving men clothed in the short tunic of their class.

In the Dark Ages we can be pretty certain that the waiter disappeared, together with all the other amenities of life. But he emerges again in Saxon times.

In early illuminated manuscripts we catch some fascinating glimpses of kings and nobles at table. The Luttrell Psalter, for example, shows us every detail of the fourteenth-century feast from the cooking of the meal to its presentation at table. The serving men wear very simple garments. Once more it is the tunic, but this time the legs are clothed in not very well fitting hose. In later medieval times everything becomes much more elaborate, and it almost seems from some of the illustrations that those who serve at table are as gorgeously clad as those who sit at meat.

There is, however, an explanation for this. In the fourteenth and fifteenth centuries waiters were often not so much the servants of the king or great lord as the boys and young men of noble family who had been sent to acquire the education of a gentleman in some court or castle. And in those days the education of a gentleman included the art of carving, for which the most elaborate rules are laid down in the books of etiquette. To be able to 'untruss a heron' was as important as to learn to break a lance.

In the sixteenth century serving men in the proper sense appear again, and soon afterwards we begin to notice that curious development of waiters' costume the principle of which has persisted until our own day. It can be summed up by saying that waiters at first wear (a perhaps simplified version of) the clothes of their masters, but that their clothes tend to change less quickly. Soon there is a perceptible time-lag. Those who waited on Louis XIV, for example, were still wearing the trunk hose of Henri IV. In the early years of the eighteenth century waiters wore the clothes of the seventeenth.

Perhaps it is misleading to use the word 'waiters' in this connection. There were great private houses and there were inns; the restaurant had not yet been invented. When it *was* invented, towards the end of the eighteenth century, the costume of domestic servants developed differently from that of such public servants (if we may call them so) as waiters. In other words the waiter and the footman became two quite different beings, differently clothed. And the time-lag in the dress of waiters is always much less than in that of footmen, who continued until the end of the nineteenth century to wear the type of clothes which the gentry had worn in the eighteenth.

Waiters in public restaurants in the early nineteenth century wore clothes which were more or less contemporary, but of course they went on wearing them even when the diners had given them up. If a film producer, to-day, wished to transform a restaurant into its aspect of a hundred years ago, all he would have to do would be to ask the customers to leave and the waiters to sit down at the tables.

In France, however, the waiter usually wore an apron, and this custom still persists. Indeed, the length of the apron (sometimes it is extremely long) is rigidly prescribed, and the knowing can deduce from it the waiter's place in the hierarchy of the establishment. Otherwise the line of development is the same as in England; and it might well have seemed until a very few years ago that the waiter's costume had stereotyped itself for ever. There were minor (and meaningful) variations; a black tie here, a white tie there. It was as if something had been deliberately introduced in order to distinguish the waiter from the customer, as was, indeed, often necessary.

When the once universal practice of dressing for dinner at a restaurant (except, of course, in the Grill Room) began to go out, this difficulty no longer arose, and it almost seemed for a time as if the white shirt-front and the tailcoat would ultimately become 'waiter's uniform' and nothing else.

Within recent years, however, waiters themselves have changed. They have taken a hint from the dress of the ship's steward, itself derived from the tropical kit of naval officers, and many waiters nowadays are clad in smart white jackets. The rest of the traditional costume is, in general, retained. So attractive do they look in this new uniform that it seems almost certain that the custom will spread. But whatever he wears, the waiter is still indispensable. Without him one of the greatest pleasures of life − civilised dining − would have vanished for ever.

Spring 1955

Apéritifs

Old Compton's Fancy

Old Compton was not one – but a Trinity of velvet-penned writers.

This most popular of features never failed to send each issue off to a flying start – until in 1980, after twenty-six years, Antony Wysard and Old Compton laid aside their pens together.

Here, too, the Fancy is served first to give each course full flavour.

Subject matter, ranging from St Swithin's Day to Bessarabian carpets, from the mathematics of beauty to lunar exploration and from hospitable sorcerers to La Belle Otero, the voluptuous Toast of Paris, was delightfully catholic.

Inevitably, however, it gravitated back to food and wine, the whole generously sprinkled with sage advice and admonition, exotic recipes, and a gentle humour. All served with the deftest touch.

Old Compton's Fancy, May

Being a true lover of the soil, Old Compton views with some distaste his neighbour's velvety-emerald lawns, weed-free flower-beds, immaculate hedges and blossom-laden fruit trees. Instead of inspiring him to mulching and manuring, this perfection has forced him to develop his own philosophy of gardening, a *rus naturalis* which in conversation emerges as 'allowing Nature to take her own course – untrammelled growth – beauty in every blade of grass and tendril of chickweed.'

After delicate hen-pecking, however, by both Miss Old Compton (aged five) and by Mrs Old Compton, he is occasionally prevailed upon to modify his views and spend odd mornings thrusting a lawn mower through recalcitrant clumps of wiry bents, macerating weed growths (and usually nearby plants) with an unmanageable hoe. After which effort, long glass in hand, he is wont to sprawl in a deckchair to recuperate from his labours, lulled by the murmuring bees and chirping crickets, indifferent alike to the wood-pigeons feasting on the peas and to the gentle susurration of the greenfly marshalling themselves for renewed attacks on the roses.

Summer 1962

Meals to Remember

Gilbert Harding

Schoolmaster, lecturer, *Times* correspondent in Cyprus – and policeman. Made his mark in radio as Chairman of The Brains Trust, and Question Master in Twenty Questions and Round Britain Quiz. Appeared on TV in What's My Line; wrote *Treasury of Insult*; and listed his recreations as 'talking, listening, looking and waiting'.

How often have so many of us said upon rising from a memorable table, 'That is a meal to be remembered for ever.' The memory of exact detail fades, and only the sensation of pleasure remains in the thankful haze of gastronomic recollection.

There is one remarkable meal of which I still remember every happy circumstance and ingredient. It was at Cambridge – at my own unspeakably beautiful college – 'the royal, religious and ancient foundation of The Queens' in that University.' (Two Queens, and therefore the apostrophe after the 's' if you please.)

* * *

A frequent visitor to the University, I sympathised often with the dreadful dietary customs of the war-time and post-war undergraduate. Gone were the days when college servants would bring green baize-covered trays to one's rooms with breakfast and luncheon: gone

28

were the days of proper meals (with a choice of entrée and of pudding) in Hall. Tousle-headed, bleary-eyed boys could be seen hurrying to Hall across the damp courtyards for breakfast, clutching horrid pots containing their 'individual allocation' of sugar, edible fat and jam – there to line up for dollops of dried egg on tired toast on cold plates, and to swill stewed tea or beastly 'coffee' in circumstances of squalor which the majesty of the splendid Hall could neither modify nor conceal. And much the same dreary process was followed at midday, and again in the evening. Ichabod! Ichabod!

It occurred to me that it wouldn't be a bad thing to go to some trouble to try to arrange a proper luncheon for about twelve undergraduates and one or two dons – to remind the old men of what had been and to give to the young ones a whiff of the fragrant past. Fortunately the excellent Mr Chamberlain, Master of the Kitchens, had always been a great friend of mine, and was now nearing the end of his fifty-two years in the College service.

He entered into the spirit of the thing. Enquiries were made. It was possible – just possible – to get some fresh cream: and, if I left it to him (and how glad I was to do so!) he might be able to lay his hands on a saddle of lamb. The only fly in the ointment was that it had to be luncheon. Dinner would have been so much better. But dinner wasn't possible; and eight of the boys were down to play rugger that afternoon.

* * *

So we began at 12.00 with a pleasant and encouraging not-too-dry sherry. Oysters were easy – twelve each, and since at least six of the young men didn't care for them, there were plenty to provide second-helpings for those that did. Then came Consommé Royale, with those cunning spongy tid-bits floating around in it (and just a touch of Marsala – so much better than sherry).

The next course was sheer greed. But there was more cream than we expected, and Chamberlain prepared some delicious lobster vol-au-vent. Up to now we had been drinking an agreeable Montrachet, slightly chilled and not frozen to death.

The lamb was superb. The red-currant jelly, made in the College kitchens, from a recipe suggested by Erasmus, has made me regret every red-currant jelly I've tasted ever since. The broccoli was crisp and green; the potatoes floury and virginally simple; the gravy rich and companionable. And with this unaccustomed pleasure, what better

to drink than La Tache – purple nectar from a tiny Burgundy vineyard with a heart so much bigger than its tiny acres.

Oddly enough no one wanted to smoke (I hasten to add that I shouldn't have minded if they had wanted to – meals being in my opinion things to be enjoyed and not affairs of discipline). After a suitable interval came the Crème Brulée – just the right creamy consistency under a thin pane of set burnt sugar. The true ambrosia! And with it – what better than a rich Château Climens (there is positively no need always to rely on the Château D'Yquem).

Another breather: and we were ready for Angels on Horseback – some proper cheeses and a few bottles of the excellent Directors' Bottle – a splendid port, neither wood nor vintage, but wholly acceptable, carefully chosen. The good Chamberlain had gone to great trouble to see that the coffee did not let us down. There was a little brandy for those that wanted it.

A good time was had by all. And at least six rugger sides were one man short that afternoon.

Spring 1955

Plucky Gin

Being the story of Royal Bob's arduous climb up the Social Ladder to 'the Buffet of lady delicate and courtier grand'

Lord Kinross

In all the chequered, romantic history of drinking there stands out one signal success story. It is the story of gin, an ardent spirit which rose from the gutter to take its place in the highest society as the companion of civilised man.

Gin, like some of the bluest-blooded families in English society, was Dutch in its origins. 'Dutch courage' it was, a spirit distilled from rye and flavoured with juniper berries, invented, or at least perfected, by a professor of chemistry at Leyden, in Holland, during the seventeenth century. The English troops, campaigning in the damp marshes of the Low Countries, found that this Hollands, as they called it, made them fight more bravely even than aquavit, with which they were familiar from other campaigns, and it was soon introduced into England. Juniper, in French, is genièvre, which became in Holland Geneva and in England, monosyllabically, gin.

Sold at first by the apothecaries for purely medicinal purposes – as a remedy, especially, for diuretic ailments – it was to revolutionise English drinking habits. Hitherto the English had been drinkers of ale, and to a lesser extent of wine. But when the Frenchified Stuarts were chased into exile, and Dutch King William III, with his Queen Mary and a retinue of Bentincks and Keppels, sailed over from Holland, in a Glorious Revolution, to take possession of the English throne, laws were made prohibiting the import of French wines and spirits, and gin came into its own, converting the English into a nation not merely of ale- but of spirit-drinkers. It was now distilled in Britain from home-grown corn and barley, as part of a policy to protect the English farmers. To drink gin became positively an act of patriotism, and it was even distributed to workers as part of their wages, just as wine is in France today. In forty years from the accession of Dutch William its consumption increased tenfold.

Apostrophising Sir Robert Walpole, George I's Prime Minister, a versifying distiller named Alexander Blunt wrote:

> fame reports
> That thou, with zeal assiduous, does attempt,
> Superior to *Canary* or *Champagne*,
> Geneva, salutiferous, to enhance;
> To rescue it from hand of porter vile
> And basket woman, and to the Buffet
> Of lady delicate and courtier grand –
> Exalt it; well from thee it may assume
> The glorious modern name of Royal Bob.

But he was anticipating. Gin remained still essentially the drink of the masses; it had a long way to go to reach the court and the mansions of ladies and gentlemen. And in its rise it was to undergo many vicissitudes.

For meanwhile, as even the best things will do, gin had gone too far. Its manufacture was uncontrolled, and it was all too easy for unscrupulous distillers to foist on the public cheap and bastard forms of the spirit, which were hawked in the street and from barrows, by barbers and tobacconists, in back-rooms and cellars and garrets and houses of ill-fame. 'One half of the town', so it was said, 'was selling poison to the other half,' and the rulers of England became concerned that its people were developing into a nation of drunkards.

Thus they introduced prohibition, in the form of the Gin Act of 1736 – a law which imposed so high a duty on spirits as to put them beyond the means of the retailer and thus of the man in the street. Like prohibition in America nearly two centuries later, it was a disastrous failure – and it lasted only half as long.

On the last day of freedom the mob was drunk, far into the night, largely on liquor distributed free, and the Guards were called out to prevent dangerous riots. Then the gin-shops went into mourning, draping crêpe over their signs, and 'The Death of Madam Geneva' was mourned in mock funeral processions. In fact the lady was far from dead. More gin was now sold, illicitly, than ever before – and it was worse gin, villainous forms of 'hooch' disguised as colic-water, or endowed with such fanciful names as My Lady's Eye Water, The Cure for the Blue Devils, or Cuckold's Comfort. An enterprising ex-Customs officer devised what was probably the first coin-in-the-slot machine – the mouth of a brass cat which, fed with two pennies, disgorged a measure of Old Tom gin.

The law could only be enforced by means of common informers, who were set upon, and sometimes thrown into the Thames, by the mob, and the magistrates soon stopped seriously trying to enforce it. Thus it became a dead letter, and after six years was repealed. Never again, even under the strong pressure of the temperance societies in the nineteenth century, has any form of prohibition been introduced into Britain.

Its repeal led to the gradual disappearance of the shadier distillers, and the rise of reputable firms like Booth's, which still thrives in its old Clerkenwell premises 200 years later, using, side by side with its modern equipment, an old riveted still, which dates from those Georgian times. Its proprietors were descended from an old county family in Cheshire. Thus, if gentlemen were not yet drinking gin, at least they were now making it.

At this time gin was usually drunk straight. It was not until later in the eighteenth century that the mixed drink, the ancestor of the cocktail, began to evolve – and then still only in the United States. It was through this that eventually gin was to achieve its rise in the social scale.

The word cocktail was known in England at this time; but it meant something different – usually a horse, or sometimes a gentleman, with a touch of mixed blood in him. As applied to a drink it probably dates from the American Revolution, when a tavern-keeper named Betty

Flanagan mixed drinks called 'bracers' for the French soldiery. One evening, giving them chickens stolen from the enemy for dinner, she decorated the bracer bottles with the tails of the cocks, and thus provoked the toast, *'Vive le cocktail!'* – or perhaps *'Vive le coquetel!'* for this was a mixed drink familiar in Bordeaux for some time past.

The name appears in this sense for the first time in an American periodical of 1806, defined as 'a stimulating liquor, composed of spirits of any kind, sugar, water and bitters – it is vulgarly called "bittered sling" and is supposed to be an excellent electioneering potion.' It was introduced into England around the middle of the nineteenth century by an American bartender named Jerry Thomas, of whom it was written that he 'gave the aid and encouragement of his genius to the cocktail, then a meek and lowly beverage pining for recognition and appreciation, and by self-sacrificing work in the laboratory raised it to its rightful place among the drinks. A perfect flood of new mixtures soon showered on a delighted world.'

Based on gin, they were at first, for the most part, long drinks. There were the Gin Crusta, Gin Daisy, Gin Fizz, Gin Flip, Gin Julep, Gin and Pine, Gin Sangaree, Gin Smash, Gin Sour, Gin Cobbler, Gin Shrub, and the John and Tom Collins. Tom may have derived its name from Old Tom gin; John from a celebrated waiter in Limmer's, a popular resort for refreshment:

> My name is John Collins, head waiter at Limmer's,
> Corner of Conduit Street, Hanover Square,
> My chief occupation is filling of brimmers
> For all the young gentlemen frequenters there.

So gin was, by this latter part of the century, a gentleman's tipple. Throughout the earlier part it had still been the drink of the gin palace, the home from home of the Victorian masses. Only in the Navy, at sea, had their social superiors deigned to drink it. Now it became the drink of the equally palatial but more refined American bar, patronised by the wealthier classes, of which the first was the Criterion, opened, with an American bar-tender in 1878.

The Edwardian Age saw the growth of the smart restaurant and the luxury hotel, and here gin glowed, continuing its climb into the best society. But its true social apotheosis was not reached until after the first world war. Gin had been scarce during the war, but now, despite new and higher duties, it returned in triumph to give to the Roaring Twenties the name of the Cocktail Age. The cocktail-party came into being – probably introduced into London, in the late 1920s by an American-born hostess, Madame Alfredo de Peña, to fill in for her friends the blank period between the office and dinner.

The cocktail itself appeared on the stage, served first by Frederick Lonsdale ('with a little absinthe in it') in *Spring Cleaning*, then by Noel Coward ('It's never too early for a cocktail') in *The Vortex*. It was finally elevated to the heights of literature by the poet of the age, T.S. Eliot, in *The Cocktail Party*. Gin, the once humble spirit, had, once and for all, arrived. It had reached, as prophesied, 'the Buffet of lady delicate and courtier grand'.

But Eliot reflected this later age truly. For in the play, in fact, the cocktail tends to yield its place to plain gin and water. Today it has shed the fancy sweet mixtures of the 1920s to become, as a rule, the very very dry Martini. The élite of the 1950s drinks its gin almost as straight – but twice as pure in quality – as the masses of the 1750s did, flavouring it in this later century with a mere dash of Martini which, in America, may be administered by a Vermouth spray. Thus the drinking wheel has come round full circle, achieving in the process a Glorious Gin Revolution which would surely have delighted the heart of Dutch King William III.

Summer 1959

Lay That Double Down, Babe

Specially written for all those ladies who have requested
more women's interest in *Wheeler's Review*

Patrick Campbell

I should be obliged if every lady present would put down her glass,
and make up her mind never to touch another drop. Except possibly a
toothful of champagne, if it's been bought for the express purpose of
lowering her resistance.

But all this general swigging of beers, spirits and heavy burgundies
must stop, until women find out how to do it.

Examine, for instance, the case of Dulcie – a pretty girl with a short
nose and large glistening eyes who in moments of fear resembles a
rabbit. Dulcie, absolutely sober, is just able to get around without
falling over cliffs and getting picked up by strange men. Knowing that
her appearance suggests idiocy, she has schooled herself to think
carefully before she speaks. On a good day she's able to remain silent,
after taking a look at what she was about to say. Dulcie, absolutely
sober, is a pleasant ornament and stands a good chance of getting home

in one piece. But Dulcie, after one drink, is a dead duck.

Here she comes, in through the swing doors, looking charming in a knobbly tweed suit, and a mannish little Italian shirt and she's done something to her hair so that it looks shiny and crisp and alive. She's only twenty-five minutes late. At least, she has no parcels, and that's a blessing. If she did have parcels they would contain fragile merchandise like a picture hat or gramophone records or a wickerwork basket for indoor ivy, and by the time we'd decided they wouldn't be safe on the floor or behind the bar and we'd put them in the cloakroom and then got the hat parcel out again because Dulcie wanted to look at it, a good deal of the steam would have gone out of the evening.

But here she is, unencumbered, and well worth looking at. Hello there, Dulcie! What'll you have?

I knew it. I *knew* it. She hasn't the faintest idea.

This rather rabbit-like but undeniably pretty girl comes titupping into licensed premises, and she hasn't the faintest idea what she wants to drink. 'I don't know,' says Dulcie. 'What are all of you having?'

I am in a position to provide a precise answer. 'A large gin and tonic. A Fernet Branca. Two small Scotch. A pint of bitter.'

'Oh,' says Dulcie. She considers it. 'I don't think,' she says, 'I'd like any of those.'

Well then – what?

Dulcie doesn't know. We stand there with our glasses in our hands cut off from all hope of further refreshment until Dulcie makes up her mind. But she couldn't tell you, under torture, what she would like to drink.

She doesn't, it seems, really care for sherry. And gin gives her a headache. Brandy makes her heart bump and, as though it were a feat comparable to bicycle riding, she has never 'learnt' how to drink beer.

Everything slows down. And stops. Everyone looks at Dulcie.

It makes her nervous. It makes her so nervous that she can't even think of the name of one drink. Ludicrous fantasies like, 'A guppin and soda,' or, 'A strinchet, with ice' flick through her mind. 'Oh well,' says Dulcie, after a convulsive effort, 'I'll have a gin and lime.'

The barman doesn't even have time to put his hand on the bottle. 'No, I won't,' says Dulcie. 'I'll have a sherry.'

The barman is a fool. 'Light, or medium, madam?' he asks, and puts Dulcie right back where she started. She doesn't know. 'Is the light,' she asks tentatively, 'very light?' 'Well, not too light, madam.' 'Is the medium sort of – more than medium?' 'Well, no, madam – it's –

medium.' If you put the question to him quickly the barman wouldn't be able to tell you his own name.

In the end Dulcie says she'd like a glass of white wine. The barman is within an ace of asking her what kind of white wine, but just checks himself in time. He looks as if he'd stepped back off the railway line a split second before the Flying Scotsman whipped by.

Five minutes later Dulcie is drunk. She is drunk in the sense that she can't find her lighter, which is on the bar in front of her. She is drunk in the sense that she has no hesitation whatever about accepting another glass of white wine. She is also drunk in the sense that her bag has slipped off her knee twice and the second time, when it was given back to her, she said, 'That's not mine, is it?'

She sits on her stool at the bar with a slight, mad smile, smoking heavily and looking round her – while she's being spoken to – with eyes that have already begun to work independently. And she can't, in common politeness, be left out of the next round.

To the terror of her gentlemen friends she says she'd like a Pernod, or something like that. The white wine wasn't very nice. She wants something to take the taste away.

Why not sherry?

'I don't like sherry,' Dulcie says, and her bag slides off her knee again. She watches gravely while one of the men picks it up. She puts it back on her knee in the same position as before.

Suddenly, she begins to talk. It comes without warning, like a dam bursting. 'Why do you want to talk about motor-cars?' Dulcie says. 'Dirty old motor-cars. You're always talking about motor-cars. Why don't you all talk about something interesting like – anything interesting ...'

'What – what sort of thing?'

'Politics,' Dulcie suggests. The cigarette has fallen out of her holder and is smouldering on the floor. 'Or something interesting. Why do you have to keep talking about motor-cars? Motor-cars are only motor-cars.' She picks up someone's whisky and drains it. 'Oh,' she says. 'How awful. That's sherry.'

'No. It was my whisky.'

'Well, then,' says Dulcie, 'where's mine? I was drinking something.' She is irritated by these foolish confusions. 'Do we have to sit here for ever?' she asks. 'Couldn't we go and dance somewhere, or have dinner, or do something. Where's my bag?' Owing to the independently sprung eyes she has addressed this remark to a total stranger, passing by. She focuses on his retreating back. 'Who's that?'

she asks. 'I know I've seen him before.'

The gentlemen friends make no attempt to answer. They cannot, indeed, pick out a question that seems answerable. They can only agree with Dulcie that it's time they moved on.

'Couldn't I have a sandwich?' Dulcie says. 'I didn't have any tea.'

Everyone sits down again. Dulcie won't have another drink – only a sandwich. 'That gin and lime's made me feel sick,' she says.

There is no point in telling her she didn't have a gin and lime. Or that sandwiches are not served at this bar. There is no point in telling her anything. And her bag has just fallen on the floor …

That's the sort of thing you get when women start dipping their beaks. I'm surprised more don't get killed.

Summer 1955

Woman and Wine

Joan Oliphant-Fraser

There are occasions, when besides looking like a sex bomb, we want to look intelligent as well. This can be achieved by discreetly (providing the type is big enough) carrying a copy of *Das Kapital*. A serious book of this calibre nicely belies the masculine image of the dumb blonde or dotty brunette.

Under the 'body beautiful' stirs an intelligence. Neath the intelligence lurks a woman with critical perceptibilities. To become a discriminating connoisseur on a particular subject is an asset. And what better subject than gourmandism. The study of food and wine pleases the body as well as the mind.

Brillat Savarin, in his book, *The Physiology of Taste* describes such a woman. ' ... There is no more charming spectacle than a fair gourmand under arms; her napkin is prettily tucked in; one hand rests on the table; the other conveys to her mouth delicately cut morsels, or a wing of partridge for her teeth to sever ...'

Or, paraphrased in a more modern idiom: 'There is no more charming spectacle than a lady oenologist as she gracefully lifts the glass up to the light to see more clearly the colour of the wine. Her well-shaped little nostrils quiver with excitement as they inhale the bouquet, followed by an expression of ecstasy as the wine trickles around her mouth before flowing down her throat ...'

A woman can become an oenologist, a bacchanalian nymph, a student of wine; though for years men have tried to keep women out of this near-exclusive male stronghold.

Oenology has been described as 'one of the pleasantest educational pursuits known to man (or woman)'. It is certainly not a difficult subject to like, especially if one has sufficient opportunity of practical work. However, as my professor said, 'when you have to taste many different wines it is fatiguing for the mouth.' This is a form of tiredness many of us, unfortunately, are seldom subjected to.

The best way to learn about wine is by following the formula evolved by Horace, that epicurean of antiquity, which was known as COS: *Colore, odore, sapore.* The eyes assess the colour, the nose the smell, the tongue and palate the taste. The senses send their reports to the brain, which is working at full strength to co-ordinate these messages. The brain then turns to its reference library where is stored and correlated the details of every wine experienced. It is then able to assess the findings of the senses, and by comparison with previous wines of similar characteristics and types, is able to arrive at a considered judgement.

When you hold a wine up to the light to look at the colour, what do you see? Is it like looking into the fortune-teller's crystal ball – cloudy and turbulent? In which case, pour it down the sink. Or is it clear, bright and brilliant? Do you see reflected the light gold of the Rheingau wines? The pale yellow tinged with green of the Chablis? The rich red robe of a Burgundy, or the lighter red of a Claret?

Select your glassware carefully. Coloured or ornate cut-glass would detract from the natural colour of the wine, so a clear, transparent glass is best. In many parts of France a tastevin is used. At a restaurant in the environs of Paris, I ordered what I thought would be a fine white Burgundy. The proprietor obviously thought so too. He reappeared with the wine and his own silver tastevin, a happy look of expectancy on his face which increased to Cheshire Cat proportions after his personal degustation.

'Have tastevin – will travel' might be adopted by discerning women. It could be either concealed in a capacious handbag or worn decoratively around the neck. As it dangled in the cleavage on a handsome ribbon, it would act as a reminder to a supine host that you do imbibe.

Don't be afraid when smelling or 'nosing' a wine to dip your beak well into the glass. Aromas are sometimes light and elusive, so it is necessary to centralise the power of concentration into the area of the nose.

The original bouquet, characteristic of young white wine, is particularly apparent in some German Moselles, the Traminer and Gewurtztraminer of Alsace and the Pouilly Blanc Fumé of the Loire: a grapey, flowery perfume, anxious to please.

M Paul Reboux, a member of the Academie des Gastronomes, likened the white wines from Bordeaux to 'liquid amber, essence of sunlight, diffusing its subtle power. The man who tastes you', he enjoins, 'will soon be oblivious to all other joys ...'. This is pretty strong competition, but if a man is more enamoured of his wine than of you, then there is only one thing to do. If you can't fight 'em, join 'em. You too can discover the 'sweet, noble, musk-scented wines of Barsac and Sauternes, peerless in savour, in perfume and richness ...'

Light and young wines are best tasted by several, generous, lingering swallows.

A Château Margaux has been compared to a full, rounded, well-packed, eighteen-year-old bosom. The man whose imagination and tastebuds were so inspired, then went off to share this superb wine, not with the palate pertaining to the bosom, but with the palates belonging to three hairy, masculine chests! Men respect a man's knowledge and appreciation of wine, and I think if we are given the opportunity to shine in this sphere, they will admire our palates as well as our bosoms.

One of the greatest compliments paid me was by an unknown Frenchman. Lunching at an unassuming but serious eating place in

Paris, my companion and myself were engrossed in discussing the merits of a partridge and several burgundies with the patron, when the Frenchman at the next table, pausing in the mastication of his chicken leg, said to his companion, 'Cette femme là,' and picking up his wine glass, added with feeling, 'je voudrais bien manger avec elle'. Men have wanted to sleep with me, but it was the first time that one ever said with such emotion that he wanted to eat with me.

If you are tired of being regarded as only 'a body to be felled at the first touch', pick up your tastebuds and become that *femme formidable*, 'a bosom with a palate'!

xxx 1967

Something Between Somethings

Countess Veronica Peel

Tapas translates into appetisers. Every bar in Andalusia has a glass shelf beneath which earthenware dishes display local specialities together with a back-up of regulars – salami, sausage, cured ham, fresh marinaded anchovies and cod or hake roes. At La Rueda (The Wagon Wheel), in Tarifa, I was introduced to a new word, *entretenemientos*, which means 'something between somethings'. And there they are really something else!

Over a copa of fino, accompanied by a dish of Caracoles (snails), my companion and I studied the menu and selection of *raciones*, or larger helpings, that are chalked up on the blackboard every day, according to season and availability. Meantime our host, José Maria, regaled us with a story about how a bucketful of these fellows had gone berserk the previous night when being coerced by his deputy into a tub of dry flour where they were meant to disgorge anything unpleasant that they might have recently consumed. He and his wife had returned home to discover that the snails had put in a considerable mileage during their absence – and spent a sleepless night rounding them up.

Eventually we ordered almejas à la cocinera (tiny, white clams) which had been frisked in wine and garlic. Angulas (baby eels) that have the consistency of fresh pasta, canaillas, those beautiful, spiky *murex brandaris* shells that gave their Greek name, *porphyra*, or its Adriatic equivalent, *porpora*, to our language in the form of purple, the dye that was extracted from them to colour the togas of emperors and the vestments of cardinals. Also navajas (razor-shells), my absolute favourite. They are simply grilled until they open and they taste sublime. Their succulent texture is similar to that of scallops and there is a surprisingly large creature inside that slim shell.

To accompany our mariscos, we ordered one tapas of Jamon de Jambugo Pata Negra. Distantly related to prosciutto and Parma ham, but cut into thicker and smaller bits, it is dark reddish-brown, with a unique nutty flavour all of its own. There are many admirable hams in Spain but this is surely the best in the world.

While our order was being prepared, José brought us tit-bits, merluza (hake) fritters, topped with pink and green mayonnaise; mejillones (before I experienced these huge orange mussels I had always laboured under the misconception that little yellow ones were preferable); gambas a la plancha; and prawns that should be eaten whole, as so much of their taste is in the shells and arms and legs.

We stuck with La Rueda's very fine fino that so perfectly complements fish. Unlike the sherry we find over here that has been fortified to enable it to travel, it doesn't leave you washed up and stranded after the high-tide has ebbed.

There is a keyhole view onto Tarifa beach, the first pure white, almost endless stretch of sand that marks the division from the Mediterranean into the Atlantic. Ships slide through the chink in endless procession, heading to and from the gateway of the Gibraltar Straits.

The inhabitants of Tarifa came and went in similar fashion, enjoying a hurried plate of delicacies such as abondigas (meat balls) at the bar, or a more leisurely racione of codornices (quails), cantollas (spider-crabs) or pinchitos (small Morrocan kebabs).

Homing in on menu items that were familiar to me, I asked José if hamburguesas (self-explanatory) and Sollomillo de Ternera (fillet of beef) were popular. He shook his head: his regulars it seems stick to ordinary, familiar food.

Our bill was 1,600 pesetas, about £7. And José gave us a bottle of red wine to take home as a gesture of his appreciation of our interest in what he obviously considers to be his perfectly unexceptional little family business.

But for me, in that tiny bar, located incongruously and elusively on the ground floor of one of a group of several tower-blocks of flats, I ate one of the most memorable meals of my life.

Summer 1983

Memorable Drinks

Allan Hall

Suggests a Little Cautious Experimentation with the
Christmas Drinks

The most memorable drink of my life was a 1976 Lafaurie-Peyraguey. It was not by any means the grandest or greatest wine of my life, although it is certainly distinguished; it was the timing of it and the circumstances of it that keep it so clear in my mind.

I had called at the château, in Sauternes not far from Yquem, with a few friends. It was, I remember a brilliant day with a slight, cooling breeze, and the pretty girls we had one way and another assembled along the way were fluttering in their delight of the old castle's enclosed garden. It was here that we were served the apéritif before lunch: Lafaurie-Peyraguey 1976, drawn from the barrel rising two years old, and chilled. It was startling, almost sparkling, you might have thought, such was its effect. The fulsome sweetness was cut by the coolness, and its freshness exhilarated us all – magicated, I think we were; one of those rare days.

Since then I've taken to a glass of Sauternes as a mid-morning drink. Nothing will recapture the flavour of that ineffable day at M Cordier's mellowed home but even in cold weather I find it uplifting. (It plays the part of a cream sherry, or a Malmsey which I often fancy at eleven of a morning – perhaps the breakfastless need the sugar.) This, perhaps, is bordering on Sauternes freakery; I can blame it only on Mr Jack Hill of Sichel, the Chief Freak in that he takes Sauternes with oysters. Try it.

Another drink I recall with gratitude is a sweet sherry with lots of ice, a generous chunk of lemon and plenty of tonic water. I was introduced to this – *una preparacion*, he called it – by the noble Gabriel Gonzalez-Gilbey. We were at the *vendimia* in Jerez when so much sherry is consumed in celebration of the harvest you'd wonder if any could be left for export.

We had planned an entire day round the vineyards and bodegas, and Gabriel had warned me that a lot of sherry would be encountered. I realised he meant it, because before we left my hotel we had done a bottle of fino between us. It's terribly easy in Jerez: two men walk up to a bar and order fino and automatically they get a half bottle. We, of course, had the other half.

The *preparacion* punctuated the endless finos throughout the day and night, hydrating, I suppose. No ill-effects the next morning, Gabriel had promised, and he was right, although the condition of the promise was that I touched no other drink but sherry. Whether the *preparacion* will work with a long day's mixture of drinks, I can't say, but if somebody cares to try it, mankind could be grateful for the findings.

The other drinking surprise that I fondly recall is the whisky lunch, devised by Wallace Milroy. It sounded a dubious enterprise, selecting four courses that made up a sane menu, each of which was particularly suited to a certain whisky. But it worked well; I think we wound up with a modest sip or two of five different whiskies, leading to Drambuie with the coffee. I recall that White Horse seemed the perfect apéritif; Glenfiddich was chosen for the cock-a-leekie soup; a fairly weighty Highland malt with the roast beef; Lagavulin from Islay with vanilla ice-cream. We had previously experimented with this and found the ice-cream had the peculiarity of drawing out the smokiness of the malt; and I think it was the majestic Macallan that led us on to the Drambuie.

So if Christmas lends you idle moments and a jaded palate, a little experimentation might prove diverting. Don't reach for the appointed drink: seek a little inspiration and listen to what your liver, a largely neglected partner in the enterprise, seems to be saying; in this way the answer will naturally present itself – sweet or dry, long or short.

But I do caution you against messing about too much with decent wines. The maker tends to follow a recipe jointly arrived at by his ancestors and God, and one should not tamper with divine inspiration.

Autumn 1983

Meals to Remember

Lord Mancroft

at last lays bare his 'Guzzle Book' to recall a varied array of unforgettable meals

2nd Baron. Educated Winchester and Christ Church, Oxford. Called to the Bar. Lieutenant Colonel, RA: twice Mentioned in Dispatches, and MBE (1945). KBE followed in 1959 after versatile spells as Lord in Waiting to the Queen (1952–54); Parliamentary Under-Secretary for the Home Office (1954–57); and Minister Without Portfolio (1957–58). Chairman London Tourist Board and Cunard Line.

Showed a fine turn of speed as Chairman of Horse Racing Totalisator (1972–76) and Greyhound Racing Boards (1977–85). And a lively sense of humour in *Punch, A Chinaman in My Bath* and *Bees in Some Bonnets*. Clubs: Pratts ... and West Ham boys.

A pillar of the Upper House.

I have just completed a ten year stint as President of the Restaurateurs' Association of Great Britain and a most enjoyable job it has been. I've met a lot of very charming and hardworking people, and I've learned a lot about a difficult and much misunderstood trade. I can also now safely release my Guzzle Book from the hiding-place where, for fear of friction, it has resided for the last ten years.

Of course, I started this Guzzle Book many years before I became connected with the RAGB; to be precise, it was whilst I was still at Oxford. This is how it works.

I've noted down over the years meals which I feel to be particularly memorable. I give them a number for food, a letter for the wine, a star for the ambience and a nominal roll of the company present.

During a particularly uncomfortable period of the war when my Regiment seemed to be eating nothing but spam and soggy dog biscuits, some of us who had journeyed together in happier times, used to compose meals from memory, just to cheer ourselves up as we shivered under our groundsheets. I myself would start with the main course – say, 27F. (This I had enjoyed at M Thulier's Oustau de Beaumanière near Les Baux-de-Provence: a superb Gigot d'Agneau en Croûte helped down with a new Gigondas.) 'Well', said my Battery Captain, 'we shall want something a little lighter before that, shan't we? What about 18K?' 'Agreed.' This was a brook trout lately swimming in its tank outside the Goldener Hirsch near Bonn (where I was studying music) escorted by a mouthful of Piesporter Michelsberg. Nice stuff.

One item in the Guzzle Book which recently caught my eye had, however, slipped my memory. Alongside it I had put both a question mark and an exclamation mark. I rang up the particular friend with whom I had shared that luncheon.

'Donald,' I said, '117Q?'

'Of course,' he replied, 'the Lygon Arms at Broadway.'

'But why the exclamation mark and why the query? What was it about that particular lunch that not only excited us but also raised certain interesting questions? Was it the Lafite 1953? Or was it perhaps that wonderful steak-and-kidney pudding with mushroom ketchup, tender spring greens and the newest of potatoes?'

'Don't be daft,' said my friend, 'it was nothing to do with the scoff. It was the waitress!'

If I were constructing my Guzzle Book anew, I would introduce a special class for mobile meals – air, sea and train. Breakfast on the 8 a.m. express out of Euston to Liverpool used to be a splendidly memorable meal. Indeed, if all British meals consisted only of breakfast we should rank high in the gastronomic league tables but, despite the welcome rebirth of the sumptuous Orient Express, British Rail are severely reducing their kitchen services in the interests of economy. Would that they would copy the Italian practice where little boys run down the platforms at major stations or, later, along the corridors, carrying baskets from which you can construct a memorable picnic.

The Russians also do this at their airports, and although most Russian food can be unendurable (they even serve raw goose in their cruise liners for breakfast) you can, if you arrive at a Russian airpoprt well before take-off, build yourself quite a useful box lunch. This practice enables the frugal Russian to dispense with a weighty kitchen in the plane and cram in a few more seats instead.

The same shrewd economic theory governs their sanitary arrangements. I was flying once from Leningrad to Kiev and I couldn't help noticing that although there wasn't the slightest sign of any turbulence, they repeatedly switched on the 'Fasten your seat belts' sign. Eventually it dawned on me that as soon as the passengers were all safely battened down in their seats, the crew had a free run of the loos. Fewer loos, therefore more fare-earning seats. Sound economics.

My first really long flight was in a BOAC Short Sunderland flying-boat bound for Singapore. The journey took five days and you came down on some romantic river every night. The food and service was excellent. Eating roast pheasant and caviare as you floated along the Arakan was a memorable experience unless, of course, you ran into a monsoon and as the planes in those days weren't pressurised, you and the pheasant were soon in trouble.

About ships I am prejudiced because I was for several years on the Board of the Cunard Line and in the Verandah Grill of the Queens they could dish up some very memorable meals indeed. I believe they can do even better now that the Seaman's Union has at last allowed a few French chefs to be shipped into the kitchen of QE2.

From French cuisine I naturally move to dear Simone Prunier who did me the honour of coming to my wedding and, in her day, ran one of the best restaurants in London.

When in 1939 war seemed imminent, it occurred to me that my Regiment, being Territorial and not Regular, had no proper cooks. The Royal Army Catering Corps hadn't been heard of in 1939, and although the raw material the War Office gave us to eat was usually excellent, the only raw material we ourselves could find to cook was not so good. Realising this, I trotted down to Pruniers and persuaded Simone to let me sign on about half a dozen of her staff as volunteers. We soon became the best fed regiment in the Royal Artillery.

But I mustn't be too rude to the poor old War Office. The beaches of Normandy wouldn't have rated many asterisks for ambience in my Guzzle Book but the twenty-four hour emergency ration pack which the Army invented to see us through the early days was a real work of art. So was their self-heating soup. You punched a hole in the lid of the tin, lit a fuse in the bottom and in thirty seconds you had a steaming plate of mulligatawny. (It was important to remember about punching that hole, otherwise the tin and you blew up).

Ambiences vary. When I was a Junior Minister at the Home Office I was made politically responsible for prisons. One day, I plucked up courage and went down to sample the food at Wormwood Scrubs. I was told to watch the prisoners' faces to assure myself the meal hadn't been specially laid on. It hadn't and it wasn't all that bad. I was glad, however, that the Governor told me after and not before lunch that the vegetable cook was doing seven years for poisoning his wife.

Very different from the Scrubs was the ambience of Wolsey's superb hall at Christ Church, Oxford, where I dined regularly as an undergraduate. Though the ambience was five star the food was, as in so many schools and colleges, seriously sub-Scrubs. It was indeed so bad that even the Dean noticed it and made an entry in the College minute book which said that since their last meeting, the Almighty in His infinite wisdom had removed Mr Bultitude, the college cook. 'If He had not done so', added the Dean, 'I should have had to remove Mr Bultitude myself.'

Meantime, we undergraduates had tried to improve matters by putting our dinner out to commercial tender. As we were only charged half a crown for our meal we hadn't much room for manoeuvre. J. Lyons & Co., however, said they would do it for two shillings – with music.

Winter 1982

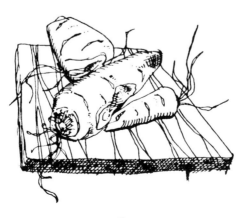

Hors D'Oeuvres

Old Compton's Fancy, February

For Old Compton the dark repulsion of this month has been cheered by the arrival from America of two sumptuous volumes – the finest examples of book-production he has seen for a long while – devoted to the role of the mushroom clan in history and in legend. Old Compton is particularly fond of edible fungi of every sort. Some which he used to gather in Windsor Forest tasted like the finest fillet steak.

Nor will he easily forget a moment in Sienna when the war had not long passed that princely city by. On the great piazza where the Palio is raced, Old Compton sat hungry and disappointed while a disconsolate ristoratore broke to him the awful news that he could expect no more than a few figs and a salad. Earlier in the day a steak had whisked through the kitchen and into the maw of a textile manufacturer from Milan. The pasta was long since exhausted ....

Suddenly, like a small angel of salvation, a tousled brown boy appeared out of nowhere with a large basket. In it glowed, golden as the hills above the Orca whence they came, the noblest specimens of *funghi porcini* – so called, it is said, from their resemblance to the pink rump of a sucking-pig – that Old Compton has ever seen. Seasoned, brushed with oil, they were soon put to roast in the oven with parsley and shallots. The result very nearly converted Old Compton to vegetarianism.

These volumes from America, however, are less concerned with fungi in the kitchen than in the poisoner's brew or the midnight incantation. They are a treasury of curious and discursive information.

For Old Compton's part, at all events, he is delighted to know that probably with the sinister-looking *amanita phalloides* did Agrippina poison the Emperor Claudius; nor is he displeased to hear that Charles Darwin's daughter, shocked by the improper shape of certain 'toadstools' in the adjoining wood, gathered them fiercely, and burnt them behind locked doors, lest the sight of them might corrupt her housemaids.

Spring 1958

Meals to Remember

Lord Killanin

Third Baron. Occupies, probably unrivalled, fifty lines in *Who's Who*.
Educated Eton, Sorbonne and Magdalene, Cambridge. *Daily Mail* War
Correspondent in Sino-Japanese War (1937-38), served throughout
World War II in 30th Armoured Brigade.

Chief claim to fame: President International Olympic Committee
(1972-80) and some twenty resultant foreign honours. Found time also
to hold varied directorships, chairmanship of Dublin Theatre Festival,
membership of Red Cross, National Lifeboat Institute, and
Thoroughbred Breeding Committees.

With John Ford directed *Playboy of the Western World*; wrote script of
Connemara and Its Pony; *Shell Guide to Ireland* (jointly) and, 1983, his part
autobiography *My Olympic Years*.

My dining room table measures twenty-one feet by five feet, seats
sixteen and is made in three sections. The third section is usually in the
baywindow overlooking the Atlantic Ocean and has been used for
generations by the children of the house. When I first ate there, and a
pince-nezed governess forced carrageen mould down my throat, I
recall the large table resplendent with silver and a fine Spode dinner
set, as a butler and two footmen served the Lords Lieutenant or the
writers of the Irish revival who would lunch with my uncle and
predecessor. Only the Spode is still in use when an occasional visitor
comes.

It is the table that is of interest, for it is of mahogany and made from
a great tree which the Atlantic storms washed off a Spanish ship on to
the beaches only a short distance from where it has been in daily use
since.

This symbol of the sea represents our daily life in the west. My
memorable meals – and I have had some exotic eastern meals with
sheiks and mandarins, expensive meals with film stars in *Romanovs* and
the *Tour d'Argent*, or simple memorable meals of fritto misto in Venice
or Tafelspitz in Vienna – have always been at home, for it is rare that
we have to eat anything which is not obtainable from a stone's throw
of our front door.

Personally, my favourite and memorable meals are Friday ones,
starting with a dozen and a half oysters from Clarenbridge with fresh
home-made brown soda bread – Galway oysters have recently been
popularised by a local festival. They are of the same tribe as those from

Whitstable or Colchester and at their best in December. Earlier, when they are small, I prefer them Mornay with a green salad, and preferably for lunch for fear they may rest on one's conscience through the night.

The main dish is hard to choose. When the first grilse and trout run, then it is a grilled salmon steak or sea trout meunière caught in my net. Their kinsmen are exported to Dublin and then maybe on to London or even the continent, but the fish which has been in the sea only a few minutes previously requires little in the way of sauces. For a change it may be a lobster and again cold and fresh rather than Armoricaine – although many of the local lobsters are flown to the Armorican coast of Brittany to be tanked until the demand (and price) is ripe in Paris; or the crayfish or langouste which I find rarely served in Dublin restaurants, with the exception of the Russell Hotel where many a memorable meal has been eaten and drunk.

Also off our coast, prawns (Dublin Bay type) which frequently masquerade in London under the name of scampi – to my mind a far inferior and insipid Mediterranean shell fish – are also found.

Although I like the whitebait which the mackerel chase on to the shore so that a muslin in my landing net scoops out dishes full, perhaps the best fish is the black sole from Galway Bay. When I am not dieting, for, being somewhat plump, this is often necessary, let me have my sole Colbert with its luscious local butter mixed with parsley from the garden. A black sole from Galway Bay rarely disappoints and, forgetting all my local patriotism, while I may have found lobster and prawns as good elsewhere, every time I eat Galway Bay black sole is memorable.

Clinging as we do on the west of the British Isles, with New York and Vigo our nearest parishes to the west and south, it is perhaps not unusual to find that Galwegians of the past drank heavily of port, claret and burgundy which was shipped direct to Galway port. The tourist will be told of the Spanish influence due to ship-wrecked sailors from the Armada, but these were few and far between compared with the daily comings and goings of the trading ships laden with wine, and returning with wool from the famed Galway sheep and a few bottles of privately distilled whiskey from the local pot stills. That influence is still to be found and I have seen trawlermen from Vigo exchanging Spanish brandy for a locally knitted woollen jersey and even a bottle of poteen. To this day good wine is to be found in local shops although my own cellar consists of a few shelves rather than bins and pipes. At the moment with my fish meals I have taken to drinking the dry Franconian wine, since a recent trip from Munich to Frankfurt, rather than the Hocks or Pouilly Fuissé, but when it is red wine I have found a very good Lussac St Emilion 1953 from a local shipper.

* * *

Not only has the silver gone to store, the footmen vanished to the grave and their liveries fed to the moth, but also the mysterious baize door has gone too. It was through this door that not only the carrageen jelly, but also Mrs Feeney's meringues, tied with blue ribbons, used to come. Quite honestly the most memorable meals are those cooked in the dining room by my wife with some critical help from myself; after, of course, I have opened the claret or sherry which has been shipped for generations direct to Galway, and unwrapped the Pont-l'Evêque type cheese from Roscommon whose matière gras appears higher and richer than those of Normandy.

Many years have passed since I first ate in the window where my children now sit with a governess, sometimes in slacks and without the pince nez; but the food is just the same, except for the carrageen jelly, and better than any I have eaten on my many trips around the world.

Winter 1959

Colchester and its Natives

It is reported that Wheeler's have recently obtained the sole concession for world distribution of Colchester Oysters ...

James Wentworth Day

Old King Cole was, as any erudite historian would inform you, a merry old soul who called for his pipe and called for his bowl and called for his fiddlers three. History, alas, does not date him precisely. He was, probably, a British chieftain or petty king who lived in bibulous state in a stockaded fort overlooking the rich, rolling countryside of East Essex, with, to the east, long miles of luminous sea-marshes and the sharp tang of the sea on the wind.

Broadly, the scene is much the same today if you disregard

motor-cars, paved streets and a population probably greater than that
of the whole kingdoms of King Cole and his neighbours.

Colchester, the *Castrum* or castle of King Cole – or Coel – has still
the smell of the sea. It is the oldest and finest town in Essex with more
history and Roman remains than almost any other town in England,
and it is the capital city of the oyster. They are, Essex men like to
think, the finest oysters in the world. King Coel, who may have been a
nickname for Cunobelin, the first recorded British king of the place,
almost certainly swallowed them. Englishmen have gone on
swallowing them ever since. The Romans, who built their great city
there under Claudius, in AD 49-50, loved them. The foundations of
their villas are peppered with oyster shells. The oyster is still king – the
true 'native'.

* * *

The oyster country lies ten miles due east of Colchester. You take the
road to Mersea Island. Eight miles on you will come to an ancient inn
with a wavy rose-red roof called The Peldon Rose. It has crouched by
the roadside for the last 400 years. Within living memory, the
smugglers dropped their barrels of French brandy into the duckpond
beside the inn and sank them in a deep well-like hole in the middle of
the pond. When the Customs men dragged the pond their grapnels
skated harmlessly over the mouth of the submarine well.

A quarter of a mile down the road the tides glitter. The saltings on either side are purple with sea-lavender. Curlew whistle and sea-swallows plunge like plummets into the shining tide. A long causeway cuts straight as a sword across the saltings and across the sea channels which for centuries have made Mersea an independent isle of infinite guile. This causeway is the strood, first laid down by the Romans. They built a lighthouse on Mersea and sent their sick and wounded there to regain health on a diet of Colchester natives. When the Romans went the Danes came. They built a stockaded camp near West Mersea church, six acres in extent. Hasten, the Dane, laid up his ships there, and raided, burned and slew for miles inland, a thousand years ago.

Here in a garden you may see still the wheel-like foundations of a great Roman lighthouse which shed its fitful gleam over the blue tides of summer and the grey and running seas of winter, when the grim fort of Othona across the estuary was a stronghold of the count of the Saxon Shore. He garrisoned it with a troop of Stablesian horse and, in these creeks and seaways, his triremes lay at anchor or thrashed seaward under banked oars, the Roman eagles at their bows.

So, you see, it is an isle of history. It is also the Isle of the Oyster. They have cultivated and dredged the oyster in these Essex seaways with much the same methods and very much the same tools that they used when the centurion sat at meat here, his slaves opening oysters with the speed and dexterity with which that longshore gunner, and fisherman, Ted Milgate, opens them today in 'Mrs Hone's' club, where you get the best food in Essex.

Most of the 'layings' or sea-bed farms are worked by families, some of whom have been on the island for anything between two centuries and what you like to guess up to 1,000 years.

Some, I do not doubt, have Danish blood. Others, like the Mussetts, originally de Musset, came over with the Huguenots after the Revocation of the Edict of Nantes in 1685, and some, like Ted Milgate's ancestors, were Bretons from the rocky bays which echo forever the Atlantic thunder. Others, like the forbears of old 'Admiral Wyatt', who died well after his ninetieth year, came long ago from the south country. An island full of history and native aristocrats. Their forebears were pirates and smugglers. But the oyster is the oldest native aristocrat of them all.

Hearken to the words of one old oysterman, a man of oyster wisdom. 'Them owd Romans started the oyster business about here an' we've kep' all on ever since. A rare owd trade – allus at it, come wind, come weather, month in, month out. Ice is our enemy. So is hot weather. Then we've got the limpets an' tingles an' the five fingers and the crabs, allus ready to kill the oyster. We don't have much spare time. An' Government don't pay us any subsidy. Yet up in London they keep all on hollerin' for Colchester Natives.'

I have known for many years most of that sea-weathered brotherhood of men who dredge for oysters, cultivate and nurse them like children in the bitter, shoaling waters that lie between the Crouch and the Colne. Their faces are graven finely by winter winds, burned by summer suns. They toil on the freezing muds of January, bake in the refracted heat of midsummer suns, and sail their clinker-built smacks where autumn gales curdle the spumy creeks.

Theirs is almost the oldest trade on earth, one with the fowler, the hunter, and the farmer.

Summer 1967

Capers in Vinegar

Monya Danischewsky

Maid of Athens, ere we part,
Give, oh, give me back my heart.
And return from 'neath thy sweater
That Incriminating Letter!

* * *

When lovely woman stoops to folly
And finds too late that men betray
She litigates – receives some lolly –
And lives to stoop another day.

* * *

Parting is such sweet sorrow ...
(I'll ring the other girl tomorrow).

Autumn 1958

John Francome – Cod Slicer

Peter O'Sullevan of the 'Daily Express'

Patrons of the Covingham Fish Bar in Covingham Square, Swindon, are familiar with the dapper figure of ex-jockey Bill Shoemark.

Finally 'grounded' after a series of injuries which are the occupational hazard of his profession, Bill has turned his attention from horseflesh to codflesh – working daily at the popular bar he owns in parnership with John Francome.

As for John himself, current champion for the third time and widely regarded as one of the most outstanding riders in the history of steeplechasing, his opportunities for preparing fish for frying are limited by demands on his more acknowledged skills.

As far as one customer is concerned this may be considered no great disadvantage.

Putting in his once-weekly appearance recently, the co-boss was detailed to slice defrozen cod at the appropriate angle.

Characteristically telling the story against himself, the horseman supreme, who has never had a riding lesson in his life and yet before his sixteenth birthday won the Young Riders' Championship of Great Britain at Hickstead, began slicing in the approved manner.

'You are supposed to get three five-ounce cod pieces out of a fish,' says John who, like his celebrated counterpart on the level, Lester Piggott, has a reputation for resolute conservation of his financial resources.

'Well, after a while I found I was getting four or five pieces out of a single fifteen-ounce fish.'

Commenting on his handiwork that evening, a customer observed forcefully, 'Look, mate, I've eaten through all this batter and I haven't found any ... fish yet. Just because you jockeys aren't allowed to eat, it doesn't mean that the rest of us have got to starve!'

Winter 1981

With Perfect Breeding ...

John Pudney

With perfect breeding does the oyster breed!
(I looked it up in the encyclopaedia)
It puts to shame the sort of life I lead,
Yet for each dulcet mouthful leaves me greedier.

What perfect breeding, in a moon-fed surge,
Tidal twilight, silty bedding, sweet discretion,
Is demonstrated by the oyster in its urge
To leave its mark – without undue impression.

Oyster, oyster, so well bred, so blameless,
Ever obstinately too discreet to utter
Mutest love song, but adept at nameless
Convolutions – join my bread and butter.

Spring 1955

Cordon Bleu

Carole Walsh

Daughter of Bernard Walsh, Carole Walsh trained with Madame Brassart at her Paris *École de Cuisine*; worked at the Ivy, the Dorchester, the Pyramide at Vienne, and all of Wheeler's restaurants, before managing the Braganza. With her husband (Ronnie Emmanuel, Joint Managing Director and later Chairman of Wheeler's), she opened the George and Dragon. Always found time to spice the Review's Menu.

Now owns and runs the lovely Thameside French Horn hotel and restaurant at Sonning.

I am giving you two recipes which can be made with Colchester oysters at around £6.00 per dozen, or Pacific or Rock oysters at around £3.00 per dozen, or Clams at £1.20 per kilo.

Oyster Soufflé

> 12 medium-sized oysters
> 2 small whiting
> 1½ oz flour
> 2 oz butter
> 2 tablespoons cream
> ¼ teaspoon of anchovy essence, or lemon juice if preferred
> 3 large eggs
> pepper

Skin the whiting, remove the bones and pound or blend.

Open the oysters, keeping the liquor. Make a roux with the butter and flour. Add the milk and liquor from the oysters. Whisk well and simmer for a few minutes. Work in the egg yolks and the purée of whiting, and anchovy essence or lemon juice, and mix well. Whisk the egg whites and fold into the mixture.

Pour into a well-buttered soufflé dish and set in a pan of water. Cook in a medium oven for 45 minutes. If you prefer, turn the soufflé out of the dish and serve with the Old Compton (tomato and fish) Sauce.

Grilled Oysters with Shallots and Butter

Open the oysters and leave on the deep shell. Chop finely the shallots and sprinkle over the oysters. Put a medium-sized knob of butter on each and place under a hot grill for about 5 minutes, depending on the size of the oysters.

Cold Crab Omelette

> 4 eggs
> 10 oz crab meat (fresh or frozen)
> 2 tablespoons of mayonnaise
> 2 tablespoons of whipped double cream
> 1 lemon
> paprika
> ½ pint milk

Prepare the crab meat. This can be brown and white or white only. Put the crab in a bowl and add lemon juice, a little paprika, and the cream and mayonnaise.

To make the omelettes, put the yolks of the eggs in a bowl with salt and pepper to taste. Beat well, adding the milk. Whisk the egg whites until stiff and fold into the yolks and milk.

Heat an omelette pan. Pour in a little oil, draining off any excess, and make a thin omelette. When cooked, put on a sheet of greaseproof paper to cool.

When you are ready to use them put the filling in the centre and fold in the usual way. Decorate the tops with cucumber, tomato and mayonnaise.

Old Compton Sauce

> 4 oz butter
> 4 oz flour
> 1 small clove garlic
> 4 oz tomato purée
> 1 small onion
> bay leaf
> thyme
> 1½ pints fish stock (sole bones only) cooked with a bay leaf and celery only.

Melt butter and add sliced onion and crushed garlic. When brown, add flour. Let it all simmer for a few minutes.

Add the fish stock, tomato purée, bay leaf and a sprig of thyme. Simmer for half an hour and remove from heat. Liquidise or put through a sieve.

This sauce can be kept in a fridge for 2-3 days and may be laced with brandy and cream before serving.

Autumn 1981

Spring Fermentations

with some notes on the Wearing of White Wines

William Younger

In the sack a young man's fancy lightly turns to things of spring. The
sack may be disappearing. If so, it is a pity. It is the one modern dress
which has stretched the male imagination almost to breaking point.
Inside it, clearly, is a woman – mobile, mysterious, maddening. But
what shape of woman? The face is there: the rest is fancy. The slippery
restless garment gives the impression either that she is an anaconda
dressed for an intimate Ascot or that the sculptor hasn't finished what
lies beneath. In this decade of do-it-yourself it is for the imagination to
complete what the sculptor has left undecided. To each man his own
Aphrodite.

   To each man also his own Sack, alcoholically as well as aesthetically.
The Elizabethans liked theirs sweet and Jack Falstaff occasionally
drank his with 'a toast in't'. This latter custom was still in some vogue
at the beginning of the eighteenth century when the Lord Mayor of
London and his officers drank sack and ate cakes 'as bigg as a crown

piece' at the Lord Mayor's Show. In 1709 a hunting squire at Windsor tried to revive the health of his bay mare with sack, but the potion failed. Perhaps the mare did not have a sweet tooth, for the equine amendment was almost certainly done with a sweet sack. This predilection for sweet and heavy sherry lasted in England until late Victorian times and it was not until the 1970s that the lighter, drier, more delicate wines of Jerez were drunk by the English. Even now they remain partly faithful to Elizabethan fashion and continue to drink a quantity of sweet sherry.

The Horse's Mouth

I suppose they no longer give sherry to horses but I am told that in Ireland a loaf of bread soaked in port is sometimes fed to a nag to hot up its performance. Jack Mytton, that reprehensible character who spent much of his life absent from sobriety, used to give his horses a couple of pints or so of warm beer, which was probably the least of his follies. I am not aware of any research made into the respective performances of horses fuelled on port, sherry, and beer. Until experiments of this nature, if made, were completed, tabulated, analysed, and published, racing of this type would add gastronomic interest to the discussion of Form and the adjustment of handicaps. The staying power given by Fino or Oloroso might have to be weighed cautiously against the propulsive qualities of 1927 and 1935 Port. The scope for advertising is obvious.

I have never seen an intoxicated nag but I have seen a horse that was about to ferment. It was a Champagne horse at Cramant, in the Côte des Blancs. This happy animal had just brought in a load of white Pinot Chardonnay grapes from the vineyards and was standing before the pressing shed. The courtyard was crowded with men, barrels, and deep, oval baskets packed tight with grapes. Into one of these the horse had dipped its snout (my knowledge of horse language is limited) and was eating with steady relish until stopped by an angry buyer. In the interests of truth I must add that the Chardonnays were not actually fermenting but a barrel of must which had just been run off the pressoir was already in ferment and frothing from the open bunghole.

I have also seen a pig full of wine, though not of sherry. This prompts me to observe that 'Sack' does not come from *saco*, one of the many Spanish words which can mean a wineskin. The pig was in northeastern Portugal and it was being carried up a mountain on a peasant's shoulder. It was, of course, headless and had been hollowed out and, in this metamorphosis, was living a second existence as an enormous, bloated bottle. It was so full of wine that it had no flexibility. Hence its charm lay merely in the nature, and not also in the mobility, of its contents. It thus emphasised one of the vital points about a sack dress, which is that the sack should not be too full. Its uncomfortable distention seemed to illustrate the Portuguese word for a drunk, a *borrachao*, a man who habitually transfers into himself too much of his *borracha*, or leather bottle.

The most delightful of Portuguese intoxicant expressions is, however, *bebado como um cacho*, drunk as a bunch of grapes, which brings me back, I suppose, to my horse at Cramant and the Beauty of Blanc de Blancs champagne.

For the Tempting Look

It is rare for any host to offer you a choice of champagne: which, considering the cost, is reasonable. But it is also rarer than it should be to find a host imaginative enough to vary his white wines according to the weather. Like suits, hats, and dresses, white wines are wines to be worn.

For a spring day *Blanc de Blancs* champagne: cool, clear, pale and delicate, but not to be drunk at evening for it is a daylight wine; nor should it be asked to please when there is a cold wind, nor under a dull sky, nor even in the bright obscurity of lamplight. Then again, the man who will give you a glass of Old Champagne before dinner is even rarer than old champagne itself. The difference between the older wine and the perpetual wedding champagne is the difference between a prima ballerina and an energetic club bore, and when you find a man who prefers the ballerina, do not let him out of your sight. It is both unwise and wasteful to leave him to be trapped by your less appreciative sisters.

For a hotter day or a summer night, for the tempting look and the tempted feeling, Pouilly-Fumé can be worn. Slightly smoky, very attractive, it is the only white wine of the Loire with a wicked edge to its charming personality. By comparison the white Pouilly-Fuissé from the Mâconnais has fewer wiles and good burgundies. The white Mâcon does too, but it can be worn casually; and neither of them, of course, demands to be treated with the distinction of a Corton-Charlemagne from the Côte d'Or.

This dignity persists further south in the white wines of the Rhône valley, in the white Hermitage and the white Châteauneuf-du-Pape.

They are strong, frank wines though sometimes, in some of the châteauneufs, for example, there is a springlike bouquet whose gaiety tempers their good breeding. Somebody once propounded an inverted theory of evolution, holding that fish were a late creation invented specifically to go with the white wines of Burgundy and the Rhône. Apart from history, the view is sound; but, adding another 'apart' – apart from hot beef and hot mutton – one can go pleasurably further and drink them with pleasure with anything.

Informal Occasions

For the less formal gastronomic attire there is the white wine (the still one) from Arbois in the Jura, though its extensive repertoire does not, to my mind, include oysters. And if you wish to dine in plate armour, there is, if you can get it, the famous Jura Château-Chalon, one of the longest lived wines in the world. I drank a seventeen-year-old bottle once among the mountains of its homeland and it had all the incisive charm of a ploughshare. Since it needs sixty years to become a fine wine, my rebuff was not surprising. At least it had one of the qualifications for a sack: it had a body which one could not ignore.

Spring 1959

Vestry Soup-Kitchen

For many years, **Gwyn Thomas**'s articles, written
with passionate Welsh *hwyl*, were as much a
delight in *Wheeler's Review* as in *Punch* itself.

The great strikes of 1921 and 1926 still operate as massive traumas in the less public parts of my psyche. In 1921 a Whitehall Napoleon dispatched a force of infantry, the Yorks and Lancs, to nip insurrection in the bud and protect the rentiers and virgins of the land from spoliation. The soldiers were small, unsoldierly and amorous fellows. Copulation throve and in our boyish games among the ferns, tripping over lovers and the attendant troupe of telescope-toting voyeurs became a fixed hazard. Often one would see a passionate Lancastrian being harangued by one of the miners appealing to him not to exhaust utterly the local supplies of warmth, and to revert, for pity's sake, to the role of running dog of imperialism.

Through that summer we were fed in soup-kitchens, housed for the most part, and for the extra laugh, in vestries. The diet differed from that of a gaol only in being served by smiling and splendid women. Never was the sweet tooth of youth so thwarted. Soup bombarded with monstrous doughboys was the dish of the day. And this was usually followed by a type of tough, unsugared rice pudding which was later taken over by Japan as the Mark One of their buna product, synthetic rubber.

Off and on some jesting sadist would run around the village shouting, 'Fruit salad down the vestry'. We would swoop like gulls around the gates of the kitchens and watch the conventional two acres of rice being lifted out of the ovens. This may earn me a frown from the American Senate but there was Russian money behind this flow of dainties. The miners of the Don Basin had a whip-round and sent the valleys a cheque to the tune of 'solidarity for ever'.

The lady in charge was the colliery manager's wife. She would stand on a high platform, correcting our clumsier gaffes. Of these, the most frequent was to give our digestive tract a truce in the starch-war by sculpting a doughboy into a kind of Easter Island figurine. And occasionally she would, in a very clear voice, make an announcement that cut a permanent groove in my mind. 'Children, tomorrow you will bring your forks. There will be butter beans.' In that age there were a legion of tough things. Those butter beans came about fifth.

When the 1926 battle came around I was in the county school and outside the orbit of public charity. In most kitchens, miracles of division and sharing swarmed like flies. The more astute got the middle cut of the sardine. Our earliest sexual stirrings were shadowed by so consistent a hunger that for years to come the zone's libido had a stammering tongue. The strike, begun in late spring, did not end until the autumn. The weather was flawless. Every day opened and closed like a great flower. The valley slipped back to its primal calm. The hillsides were murmurous with groups talking, singing, gambling with buttons or pins.

At school every class witnessed a bijou but solemnly bitter civil war. The miners' sons were for conflict unto death. The sons of tradesmen and other people not affected by the fight were malignantly opposed to the whole business, especially during the General Strike part of the affray, when they had to go without buses and trains. They did the long walk down the valley, working up a fine, reactionary head of steam.

Winter 1982

A Quick Dab of Cognac

or, What to give your wife for Christmas

James Campbell

Women of Madeira were among the first to appreciate that a dab of Madeira behind their ears was as attractive to men as any perfume, and in the great brandy shippers' châteaux in Jalnac the perfume bottles in the guests' bedrooms are filled not with *Je Reviens* or *L'Interdit* but with cognac.

There is little doubt that the majority of men in this country would more willingly follow in the wake of a tantalising trail of Château Yquêm than Jolie Madame, prefer a hint of Château Latour (Cru of course) to Diorama, and might conceivably find more complimentary things to say about a touch of gin at the wrist than any amount of *My Sin*.

At cocktail parties you might be seriously tempted to make an inappropriate remark to a lady who told you her perfume was *L'Heure Bleue*. How much more impressive to be able to say, 'I adore that perfume you are wearing. Let me think ... Pouilly-Fuissé 1962; No?'

Weeks of rewarding research would be necessary, both at home and in the off-licence, before you could even hope to select the perfect gift for wife or girl friends. Incomparable hours spent sniffing bouquets to decide whether Margaret, for instance, who has floated almost from the cradle on an aura of Chant d'Aromes, would be happier exuding drifts of vintage Pink Champagne or the comehitherishness of a Vosné-Romanée. Would the exotic Annabel be insulted or amused if presented with a bottle of Tiger Milk instead of your annual gift of *In Love*? Aunt Maud, who is not, nor ever has been, the lavender water type, would undoubtedly get more of a kick from Lamb's Navy Rum. She might even be so appreciative of this change of heart as to leave you enough in her will to enable you to lay down a decent cellar of your own at last.

And although when choosing a gift for a lady, money is naturally your last consideration, it is worth noting that a two-ounce bottle of *Joy* will set you back £29, but a magnum of Puligny-Montrachet première cuvée 'for her dressing table' costs only £2 10s. 6d.

Autumn 1967

Soup

Old Compton's Fancy, August

August, Old Compton holds, is essentially a month of movement, purely in search of pleasure and respite. Were he free to choose, he would be hard put to decide whether he would turn his nose northward to the burns and the bracken, the sea-lochs and the incomparable islands of Argyllshire, or south towards some aromatic glittering Mediterranean coast. In his estimation, there are few pleasures to surpass the charm of walking up grouse over dogs in the early season and when the bracken and the slopes have left you in a panting sweat, what sweeter music is there than the tinkle of some fern-clad burn where you slake your thirst on brown, cold water that tastes as fine as any Spaetauslese? On the other hand, as like as not it will drizzle interminably and Old Compton's holiday would fritter itself away in futile games of Canasta.

If he go south, on the other hand, there is the joy of the poplars flashing by and the first sight of olive groves, which Cocteau has likened to the beauty of grey hair above a young face. But when he reaches his coast, Old Compton fears he may find the rest of England there before him.

Perplexed, Old Compton turns for solace to his dinner. He proposes to start with a cold Polish bortsch. Young globe beetroot have been steeped in water, within a hermetically sealed jar, for ten days, till *kvass*, that fermentation so dear to the Slavonic world, has been formed. This is added to a good strong poultry stock, simmered for a moment or so and then chilled. At the last moment shrimps, cucumber and spring onions are added. The result Old Compton finds celestial. After he will attack a duckling garnished with tangerine salad, and washed down by a 1953 Beaujolais.

Summer 1958

Meals to Remember

Sir Compton Mackenzie, OBE

Educated at St Pauls and Magdalen, Oxford. Survived the Dardanelles to become Director Aegean Intelligence Service. Literary Critic of the *Daily Mail* 1931-35, and Editor of *The Gramophone* (1923-61). Had early success as a novelist, poet and playwright with *Carnival* and *Sinister Street*. A vast output ran through *Santa Claus in Summer* and *The Red Tapeworm* to peak perhaps on his own hearth in the hilarious *Whisky Galore*, equally successful as a film. A multifarious President: Wexford Festival, Dickens Association, Siamese Cat Club, Songwriters' Guild, Poetry Society – and Croquet Association.

About a quarter of a century ago the Wine and Food Society gave their inaugural lunch in the Connaught Rooms. We sat, as I remember, at a very large round table, but I ought to add that, such was the quality of the wine and the food upon this noble occasion, it may well be that my memory has removed all angles from what in retrospect seems a perfect circle. The dish I particularly recall was of plump autumnal quails suitably garnished with grapes, but the outstanding feature of that lunch was a Montrachet of the 1922 vintage the peer of which I never hope to meet in this mortal life and the bouquet of which remains upon my palate even to this day. At the end of this great lunch we drank two kinds of Marc de Bourgogne, which I had never tasted before and which I have never been lucky enough to find since in any restaurant in Great Britain. *Verbum sapienti.*

* * *

At one of these dinners, from which in a symphony of grey and rose I recall eating Belon oysters and drinking the pink champagne of Bouzy before we went into the salon, I had the honour of taking in Madame Cointreau, who sat between Sir Eric Phipps the Ambassador and me. Had I found the Widow Clicquot herself on my arm I should not have been more aware of an immortal name. Madame Cointreau was a beautiful blonde – half Swedish, half Scots – exquisitely dressed and a conversationalist of grace and charm. I never drink a glass of Cointreau without thinking of her on that evening in a Paris heavy with the sense of impending ineluctable calamity.

The dish that remains most vividly in my memory is grilled salmon

with anchovy butter cooked by my secretary, Christina MacSween.
Let me quickly add that it was a sauce made with real anchovies; not a
synthetic affair shaken out of a bottle. I declare without hesitation that
this is the best condiment of all with salmon and, indeed, it could be
used more often for other fish if it were not such a trouble to make.
We drank with it the best Pouilly-Fuissé I ever drank, but alas, I have

forgotten the year. It had more noticeably than in any other I have drunk the faint smokiness which gives Pouilly-Fuissé such individuality. We had Pol Roger 1928 with the poussins, but the high spot of the drink was a Cognac of 1833. It was meet and right to uncork that glorious bottle during the last few days of peace left.

Summer 1955

Shall I Compare Thee to a Glass of Wine?

Fascinating Speculations on a Twin Interest in Life

Peter Luke

As a man gets older he tends to find his interest in women becoming more academic and his attitude to wine more practical; the one in direct ratio to the other. At this time in his life when a bottle of wine becomes his first pleasure the adjectives, analogies and metaphors he uses to discuss it often become confused with those used in his more physically robust days.

The late Horace Annesley Vachell was a man who possessed great charm – and beauty; virile as he was, there is no better word to describe this kindly, elegant old gentleman. Apart from a quantitively considerable literary output he had been variously an athlete of distinction, a 'stage-door Johnny' and an officer in a crack regiment. He was *par excellence* an amateur of wine and women and towards the evening of his very long life he retired to the West Country and his cellar. It was near his ninetieth birthday that a small symposium of wine-loving friends came to visit him at his house one summer evening bringing the gift of a few bottles of a very fine, light Moselle.

The wine was cool enough to drink almost at once and the evening sun shone through the old man's nostril and his glass as he held the one fine instrument to the other. He smelt it, and sipped it – and smelt and sipped it again before, in a light tenor voice quavering with emotion, he made his pronouncement: 'It is like ...' he said, and stopped to sniff again the wine. 'Yes. It is like a very – young – girl.'

Thus spoke a nonagenarian. Younger men may be inclined to use their similies in reverse or ambivalently – according to age and enthusiasm. A knowledge of French wine trade jargon or – and here is a red hot tip for the *wein/weib* connoisseur – a perusal of a publication

called *Bordeaux et Ses Vins* gives a new dimension to the language of love. For example, the wine Mr Vachell referred to was certainly *fin*, probably rather *mince* but, without doubt, *racé*; so was that constant nymph Miss Elisabeth Bergner and so is Miss Margaret Leighton, though this implies no comparison, flattering or otherwise, between these two actresses.

But to start at the beginning, many well-found girls are *un peu rudes en primeur* a number of the post-war crop of Italian film stars, for example – but as they develop (in the literary sense of the word) they tend to become *corsé, souple* and even *coulant*. But if their evolution is extreme in the physical sense their charms can be described as *charnus* which term, since the present cult in the entertainment world is all in this direction, is not derogatory. It would be perfectly safe to say that a good Pomerol and Miss Dors had *beaucoup de corps*.

Another person who comes to mind in an extension of this wine/woman category is Mrs Arthur Miller who combines *sève* in her stage performance with *fermeté* of purpose and physique. She is a Côte Rôtie or a particularly charming Crozes-Hermitage, whereas that sleepy-looking Mlle Simone Signoret (he who hasn't seen *Le Casque D'Or* has missed, or is liable to miss, a superb visual and emotional treat) would seem to come from a little further north: Chiroubles, perhaps, or Saint-Amour. She is a Woman; a woman *veloutée et généreuse*.

A woman – again the word is used in its most complimentary sense – who has already achieved *une longue tenue* is La Magnani, a woman with *qualités maîtresses*, and no *double entendre* is intended. And among the really Grands Crus is Miss Katherine Hepburn, an actress *sèche, nerveuse et élégante*; and, of course, the great Garbo who is not quite *sèche* but how *élégante, nerveuse* and *plein de race et de distinction* like a very mature Red Graves.... One could continue indefinitely in this vein, but let that be the reader's pastime.

With this twin interest in life, this dual passport to happiness in his pocket, no man however young or old need suffer a moment's anxiety lest the best things in life are passing him by, for as one pleasure declines so does the other increase – provided he has money in his purse. A young man of sixteen recently on holiday from his public school was being quietly chided for helping himself so liberally to the Armagnac at a dinner party. He replied, 'Good Lord, Mummy, that's nothing. Mahoney and I sit on our study window-sill and drink off a three-and-sixpenny bottle of brandy at one swallow.'

At the other end of the scale, the writer's great-great-uncle, who rather resentfully shuffled off in his ninety-seventh year, gives an equally encouraging example. At his ninety-sixth birthday party, in Sacher's Hotel, he noticed an exceptionally beautiful Viennese lady pass by the table. Putting down his glass of Tokay he swivelled round in his chair the better to see her. At last, turning again to the assembled company of relatives, he drained his glass and thumped the table. 'If only …,' he said, 'If only I were eighty again.'

Autumn 1958

Highlife Springtime Romance Drama

D.B. Wyndham Lewis

'So Mary had *a little lamb*! –
   Edward! I blush for you, bydam!

Unhappy Boy!' the Duchess said,
   And bowed her haughty, stricken head.

Her voice rose to a sudden roar:
   'Your Mary is a Carnivore!

A Hockey-Girl, no doubt, at heart,
   Lusting to tear raw steaks apart!

Heir of a Vegetarian Line,
   What have you done to me, you swine?'

Lord Edward muttered in a daze:
   '*Moskova, Orsay, Navarraise,*

Americaine, or *Irish Stew* —
  Oh, Mother, if you only knew!

See, here, her portrait!'* cried the Youth,
  'Instinct with modesty and truth;

Where'er the Graces are at home —
  Antoine's, the *Ivy*, the *Vendome* —

Of all the votaries of *Wheeler*
  None can be fairer, or genteeler,

And by her side ('twas at my wish)
  Behold my angel's favourite dish!'

A mother's fears are quickly past,
  Her Grace essayed a chop at last ....

Now, with the lofty poise of yore,
  She wades into the Plat du Jore,

And scorning censure as renown,
  She swings the prettiest fork in town.

Spring 1958

*Permission to reproduce the portrait, an oil-painting by Dali now
in the Long Gallery at King's Umbrage (open to the public
alternate Fridays, 2.30—4.30 p.m.) was withheld by the Duchess.

Tax Collector of Blessed Memory

Allan Hall describes the almost religious ceremonial of bidding for the great Meursault wines at the Hospice de Beaune.

There was a time when the rich thought they could buy their way into heaven. If you had the money, a bribe for the heavenly gate-keeper was a wise investment. Thus did the great and glorious Hospice de Beaune come by its endowments, making the institution the most renowned of all the Burgundian vineyard owners.

The hospice was founded five centuries ago by the king's tax collector, Nicolas Rollin, no doubt regarded as a churl at the time but now reversed, his unseemly pursuit forgotten, his name on what usually turns out to be best red wine produced by the hospice.

The dukes of Burgundy were among the first of the salvation-seekers to give parts of their vineyards to the hospice; other hopefuls followed suit. And may we all, not just the poor and the sick who to this day are sustained by the proceeds of the vineyards, be ever thankful.

For 100 years or so the sale of the hospice wine has been formalised into a typical piece of French rodomontade. Every November, on the third Sunday, the world of wine converges on Beaune to bid for a cask, known as a *pièce*, of the finest potion known to man.

The auction is conducted with great solemnity, with all the Elders of the Burgundy wine industry in attendance. The subject matter may be wine and how many francs somebody might part with, but the atmosphere is liturgical, the bidding hushed, as in responses. The stranger might easily suppose he is taking part in an office of the church, an impression encouraged by the burning of candles to signal the various stations of the bidding.

All the years I've been going there I haven't had an inkling of what's going on. The church and the wine business have always enjoyed a bit of mystery – it blurs the edges when it comes to awkward questions – and it takes a keen, concentrated business brain to enter the bidding. The mind must not idly stray from these devotions.

An old hand began to explain it to me once: 'As I understand it, there are three wicks for each lot and as one burns down the second is started and if the bidding then stops, the last bidder gets it, and then there's a third wick, if I understand it ...', which seemed to me to demonstrate a perilously frail grasp on the thousands of francs at stake. And yet he's a chap who consistently buys the best wine at the best price!

It says much for Wheeler's reputation that these days, the French expect the chairman, Ronnie Emmanuel, to be among them every November. Wheeler's are the biggest individual buyers.

What happens is that Wheeler's great friend in Burgundy, Paul Bouchard, does an initial selection and fines down the number of wines to nine. It is from these that Emmanuel makes his decision. It is always Meursault, of course; not the red wines. In 1979 and 1980, it was the Meursault bearing the great name of Goureau; the 1981 (not yet being served) is Les Genevrières.

Even with such an abundant harvest this year, the prices are unlikely to go down. The 1980 was bought cheaply; for one of the world's great wines, the selling price of £15.50 is reasonable. The 1981 will have to be £19.90. The 1982, obviously more, but a wine of this quality is considered central to Wheeler's wine-buying policy.

'Whatever else we may keep,' it is said, 'we have three first-class house wines. Wheeler's own label from the Loire, marvellous value at £4.25; our own premier crû Chablis, specially selected for us and selling at £9.95; and the Hospice Meursault at £15.50'. I wonder who else has customers who fancy the occasional Hospice Meursault as a house wine.

Winter 1982

Quotations

The blood of grapes.

Genesis XLIX.

There is a crying for wine in the streets: all joy is darkened, the mirth of the land is gone.

Isaiah XXIV.

Wine makes old wives wenches.

John Clarke.

When the wine is in, the wit is out.

Thomas Fuller.

One barrel of wine can work more miracles than a church full of saints.

Italian Proverb.

Wine wears no breeches.

French Proverb.

Winter 1982

Beautiful, Beautiful Soup

Hugo Dunn-Meynell in his continued quest for exotic foods, describes the intriguing life-style of the turtle as well as the best ways of giving it full culinary honours.

The French have their garlicky bouillabaise, the Russians – appropriately – their deep red borscht, Americans their clam chowder. Courageous Japanese lap up a broth made from the deadly fugu fish, fastidious Chinese simmer birds' nests, and jolly swagmen's billies boil kangaroo tails – while in Spain they enjoy *olla podrida* (which, according to my dictionary, means 'dirty pot' – but that's their affair). In parts of Africa, folk still talk about the *velouté de missionnaire* of the good old days. But to us British, the ultimate soup is turtle.

No other potée, potage or pot-au-feu comes near to the comforting, rich, glutinous nourishment of that glorious greeny-brown consommé.

Madeira must have been invented to drink with it, cheese straws to be eaten with it, and gold plates to serve it in. One great English poet was so impressed by his first bowlful that he sat down and penned an epic of lament that he had only one stomach to fill with the nectar. (If you don't believe that, just look up 'turtle' in the *Oxford Dictionary of Quotations*).

How it has come about that the one essential dish at every Lord Mayor's banquet in the City of London is made from the reptile which inspired both military tank and submarine is a bit of a mystery. But so are many things about the turtle.

In the first place, you cannot make soup from any old shellback. There are nearly 300 different species, many of which live on land and are easy to catch because they cannot flee fast enough; but perversely these won't do. What is needed is a full-grown sea-turtle, and they have always been very hard to get hold of.

The trouble starts before the reptile is even born. Turtles are found throughout the tropical seas but, for a large proportion, 'home' means one of the Galapagos Islands or the Seychelles. However, parent *chelloniae* tend to travel rather great distances on honeymoon, and it is not uncommon for the bride to find herself pregnant 1,000 miles or so from home. The tradition is for expectant turtles to make their way back to the very beach where they themselves were hatched – though how they manage the navigation is a complete mystery.

On arrival, somewhat exhausted, the mother digs a pit in the sand, lays her eggs, buries them, staggers down to the sea and returns to the flippers of her impatient spouse (spouses usually: there's something about young turtles that makes them specially popular with the neighbours). The hot sand incubates the eggs, and in due course a lot of little turtles scramble up and set off for the water.

Here are more problems. The news of hatching spreads fast, and just about every species of fauna for miles around comes rushing to the scene. Of course, they arrive too late to congratulate the happy parents who – to quote the advertising – are already at work on an egg. So the visitors decide to have a snack. Now coyotes and crabs find baby turtles very appetising – rather like Cornish pasties with exceptionally tough pastry. The result is that relatively few infant turtles get as far as the sea. Those who do make it meet all sorts of new hazards, from sharks to lobsters. The turtles which survive this stage will grow to a considerable size – seven feet or so in length, with an even greater span. Thereafter, the lobsters at any rate keep their distance, and even sharks tend to prefer other delicacies (human legs, and so on) to those hard shells.

Until deep-frying came along, the best soup was made from freshly killed beasts. The Lord Mayor's Seychelles ambassador shipped them live in tanks to the Port of London. His chefs made matters more difficult by insisting on females: this posed another problem, since turtles do not flaunt their charms like some other species I could mention, and it took considerable patience for a fisherman to discover whether he had found the lady. Ogden Nash summed it up rather well when he wrote:

> I think it's clever of the turtle
> In such a fix to be so fertile.

Captive turtles evidently had a pretty good idea of the reason for their voyage, because the moment they were landed they all pulled their heads in and pretended not to be there at all. Rotas of junior chefs took turns waiting for heads to pop out again. I will draw a discreet veil over what happened then; I find it gruesome. But things did at least get simpler. Turtle soup is, after all, quite easy to make once you have a huge supply of the meat and about ten hours to spare.

There are a good many versions of the classic broth, none of which (in my limited experience) rivals the Guildhall version; but I suppose City Elders can get bored with the same old feast night after night. For such jaded palates, I recommend Lady Curzon Soup — a basic consommé enriched with thick cream, curry and a lot of sherry. Her Ladyship invented it to comfort her husband when, as Viceroy of India, he found himself obliged to entertain teetotal guests.

If a chef ever does get hold of some turtle meat that has not been earmarked for the Guildhall stewpot, there are several other ways he can use it. Its steaks are excellent grilled, or marinated in lemon juice, sautéed, and stewed in a casserole with carrots. Or the meat can be cut into pieces for an original and delicate kebab. Escoffier recommended braised flipper au madère; Prosper Montagné favoured recipes à l'américaine (in a lobster sauce), à la financière (with truffles), and even using cucumbers. Some unsporting gourmets have been known to eat turtle eggs, which look exactly like golf balls — a fact that makes it very easy to give the cads their come-uppance on 1 April.

Inevitably, the French credit the turtle (as, in my experience, they do any costly food) with aphrodisiac qualities, from which both sexes (of the French I mean, not turtles) are reputed to benefit greatly. The more down-to-earth Roman poet Pliny claimed that turtle meat cured toothache.

In 1979, private fishing for wild turtles became illegal all over the world, and anyone wishing to import turtle meat must, nowadays, obtain a special licence to buy it from the turtle farm in the Cayman Islands. Although the conservationists are still not completely satisfied, it does seem that the danger of this graceful prehistoric beast becoming extinct has passed. Otherwise, turtle soup would disappear into history like Apicius' ragoût of song-birds' tongues, Cleopatra's pearls dissolved in wine and Stephen Gaselee's spiced buffalo hump. As it is, a few English firms make soup for us with the frozen meat, and very good it is too. Of course, like all the best things it gets more and more expensive.

Mrs Beeton anticipated the problem a century ago and devised a recipe for Mock Turtle soup — using a stewed calf's head to simulate the gelatinous characteristics of the real thing. And shortly afterwards, John Tenniel, the illustrator of *Alice in Wonderland*, drew a mock turtle. One can fairly say that it resembles a turtle just about as nearly as the recipe tastes like turtle soup!

Winter 1981

The Gloomy Gourmet

– after visiting a recent Food Fair
(with profound apologies to Christopher Marlowe)

V. Morley Lawson

Come dine with me, and be my guest,
And we shall some new dishes prove;
Of fishless fish that ne'er saw sea,
And meatless meat that ne'er saw hoof.

A soup that the Medicis praised;
But have no fear t'will spread your waist;
It's only water added to
Four grammes of concentrated paste.

From San Francisco's sun-drenched bay,
(Or thereabouts) a clamless chowder.
Rice starch, glumate and cotton waste
Smooth blended with a dried fish powder.

But stay, there's wine to grace the feast.
'It's years ahead.' superb! Alive!
Red, white or sparkling – as you wish,
'ICI 1965.'

And now in chop or sirloin shape
(And only ninety secs. to bake)
By-product of a sawmill's waste.
A tenderised leaf-protein steak.

A sweet defying all description;
Of almond essence, pectin, pods,
Fruit acid, colours, saccharine.
A Gâteau! What a feast for Clods!

Winter 1960

Fish

Old Compton's Fancy, January

Planets and celestial portents are not enough for Old Compton's foreshore forebodings. Starfish, prawns, lobsters, crabs and all sorts of crustaceous combinations have great significance in his astrology. A steamed Dover sole in white wine sauce, with shrimps, oysters, mussels and mushrooms (known as Sole Marguery) means a great deal to Old Compton. It means even more if it is found in heavenly conjunction with a bottle of Pouilly-Fuissé.

These happy omens are interrupted by Taurus, the Bull, rising in the full moon chart for England in January. This means that there will be important news regarding food problems and difficulties. These can be ignored only at the risk of unwelcome developments which may lead to compulsory dieting and enforced abstemiousness. Old Compton combs the beaches to solve your problems and save your digestion.

Were you born between 21 December and 20 January? Your sign is Capricorn or the Goat, which is on the map but off the menu. Colours are oyster-grey, Stilton-blue, russet (this points to tawny port) and dark shades of brown, which suggest dark sherries or Madeira.

Spring 1955

May

Before he could say 'bain marie' Old Compton was recently whisked to a culinary academy which, though maintained by the LCC, would have won accolades from Carême or Francatelli. Never did he see a passion for detail more lovingly or nobly applied. 'The chefs of the past', nevertheless remarked one cook-instructor, 'were veritable bond-slaves to their art. We could never demand that servitude of our young people!'

Yet when Old Compton inspected the beauty of the Cornets de Jambon à la Salade Russe, or the Ballotines de Volaille, raising their swan-necks in apprehension as they went into the copper braising-pan; when he observed the lectured classes who took notes on the art of a Bavaroise aux Peches; when, furthermore, he actually experienced the school's cooking and the impeccable service it teaches its young neophytes – the whispered confidence of the menu, napkin veiling the hieratically crooked left arm – he felt that some hope still survived for Western civilisation.

Old Compton's fancy turns this month to one of those delicious young turkeys of not more than five pounds that are so plentiful just

90

now. It should be braised and preceded by gull's eggs. With the young turkey Old Compton proposes to enjoy Carottes Vichy, the only fashion in which the charming delicacy of young carrots can be truly honoured. Cut into pieces of uniform size, they are covered with cold water, to which sugar and butter have been generously added, together with a pinch of salt and pepper. They are then boiled fast in an open saucepan till all the water has evaporated and the tender vegetables braised in a syrup of sugar and butter. Now is the moment to cast in a handful of finely chopped parsley. Fried a moment with carrots, it lends to them an incomparable flavour of the spring.

With this meal Old Compton would propose to drink a Gewurztraminer 1953, which with its lingering after-bouquet is ideally suited to honour the summer.

Summer 1958

Meals to Remember

Some fascinating wartime culinary experiences around
strictly non-belligerent Dublin Bay .

Patrick Campbell

Third Baron Glenavy. Columnist *Sunday Times* and *Sunday Dispatch*, assistant editor of *Lilliput*. One of the most popular and prolific humorists of his day. Books included *A Short Trot with a Cultured Mind*, *Life in Thin Slices* and *A Feast of True Fandangles*. Charmed millions of viewers on BBC 2's *Call My Bluff*.

Six foot six, reddish haired, a Protestant Dubliner of Scots ancestry, he was the grandson of a Lord Chancellor of Ireland, and holder of an English peerage.

In *Who's Who*, listed Rossall, Pembroke, Oxford and *Irish Marine Service* as sources of his education – and golf and 'pleasure' as his recreations.

I slide my contribution into this series down a runway of cooking fats so fearful that it may well cause the customers to thrust away from them, untouched, Wheeler's plainest and most welcome dish.

I sympathise. I don't feel hungry either – not now that I am compelled to remember the cuisine of the Gooser O'Toole.

The Gooser was a hollow-cheeked, stoop-shouldered, animal-eyed youth of intermediate age who'd spent most of his formative years leaning against walls along the Dublin docks, unofficially assisting from time to time in the unloading of Guinness barrels, returned empty – but not quite – from England. The 'not quite' ingredient had the consistency of treacle and the effect – if the quantity was right – of getting the Gooser arrested on varying charges of violence three times out of five.

It will never be known why he joined the Irish Marine Service, which was hurriedly formed at the outbreak of war. An inflated conception of the wages, and the meaning of 'all found', certainly had more to do with it than his own statement – 'In Ireland's hour of need I'm ready – anny place, anny time.'

I tried hard to keep him out of my watch, and even harder to prevent him taking over the cooking, but the Gooser was too quick for me. That swift, murky eye of his for the main chance had instantly perceived that he'd be far better off down below, over a warm stove, than sloshing about in a small motor-launch, chasing coal-boats around Dublin Bay.

This was our function – to board and to search all incoming vessels, sincerely hoping we should find nothing of a belligerent nature to infringe our neutrality or – of equal importance – to terminate our lives.

The vessel from which we operated was a very small tug with a very large funnel. It looked as though it ought to be on wheels, like a child's toy. This craft had begun its career some thirty years previously, performing every kind of menial duty around the soupy, fruit-sodden waters of the Port of Dublin.

The six of us lived in an iron box aft of the engine-room, a chamber impregnated to its very soul with diesel oil, coal dust, turf smoke, old clothes, decaying rubber boots, brilliantine, and the smell of fish. The smell of fish seemed to bind all the separate components together, while bringing out the full savour of the individual parts.

In this tangible atmosphere we spent twenty-four hours every three days, anchored two miles out near the Bar Buoy, occasionally going off in the launch to board an incoming vessel and returning, then, momentarily revived by the fresh air, to be paralysed all over again by the exhaust gases of the Gooser's cooking.

He cooked in a woollen vest, bowed over a small range, the flap of which he kept wide open so that it glowed a dull red at all hours of the day and night. His only utensil was a large, iron pot which he'd swiped, as soon as it arrived, from the billet ashore. Inquiries about it went on circulating for months after its disappearance. When we went off duty the Gooser stored it for safety in the bilge, under the engine-room floor, returning it lovingly to service next time out with a quick wipe round from the strip of muttoncloth he wore like a bandage round his neck.

As soon as we'd anchored on station, at about nine o'clock in the morning, I used to go down aft and watch the Gooser unpacking and laying out his supplies. The range and the iron pot would already be at full blast, boiling water – the diesel oil gave it a rainbow tint – for the morning tea.

For our twenty-four hour spell of duty at sea we were issued, by the Army, with sufficient rations to keep a soldier alive for twelve hours on dry land. At this time the Marine Service was too new to have its own system, or source of supply. To provide a menu for the long, cold watches of the night was, therefore, the Gooser's problem. He came to grips with it ruthlessly, fining the whole thing down to an adequate supply of what he called 'grace'. By this he meant grease, although I always made a special effort in his presence to refer to it as cooking-fat.

The Gooser was a cooking-fat collector, prowling rapaciously about the billet on his day ashore. He had, it seemed, only to pass his eye over a discarded lump of suet in the galley for it to disappear without a trace. A shipmate, reaching for the jam, would suddenly find that his margarine ration, and the Gooser, had left the table at the same time. Even bacon rinds weren't safe; but the really disturbing thing was that all this loot went into the Gooser's sea-boots, for safe keeping, with his sea-boot stockings, once white, stuffed into the tops of them, like corks, to lend them an air of innocence.

That's why I used to go down aft to watch him unpacking – to make sure that the raw materials that were being tipped out of the sea-boots, wrapped in twists of newspaper, were at least in theory edible, before they lost their identity by being rendered down. The Gooser, I felt, was sufficiently fanatical about his 'grace' to add linseed oil from the armoury, if all else failed.

The first and, indeed, the only conventional meal of the day was dinner, served at lunch-time by the Gooser from his iron pot with a ladle made by himself from a splayed-out length of wire rope. It was always stew, and its preparation was simple. The Gooser roasted hell out of whatever meat we'd been given and then drained off the fat into a tin that once contained back-axle lubricant.

The primary purpose of his cooking had now been achieved, and he applied himself to the finishing touches in an off-hand manner. He sawed the blackened cannon-ball of meat into six fairly equal portions, threw in potatoes and a cabbage, still in the same condition as they had come from the good earth, topped up with sea-water and then boiled until ready. It came out pale-grey, tasted like the seat of a trawlerman's trousers, and created a thirst the like of which I have never known before.

Sometimes, when I'd been out for several hours in the launch, chasing ships all over the place, I'd return to the tug round about dawn, very cold, and famished with hunger. Then I'd cut myself a good big slice of the Gooser's stew, take another look at it, and then quietly tip the whole lot over the side.

Spring 1957

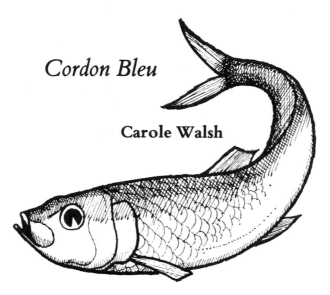

Cordon Bleu

Carole Walsh

I am meeting more and more people who are extremely concerned about their health and eating the right sort of food. I have, therefore, found some delicious recipes, with interesting variations, using yogourt instead of cream. Halibut, turbot and cod, also fillets of sole may all be cooked in this way.

I heard recently of a very good way to improve the texture of fish that is served in cutlets or steaks. Tie the cutlet so that it stays a round shape. Put it in a dish and cover it with cold water and ice cubes. Leave for one to two hours before cooking. This firms the flesh and gives it that freshly caught quality.

Baked Halibut with Fennel or Celery

> 4 halibut steaks
> 8 tablespoons natural yogourt
> 4 tablespoons finely chopped fennel or celery
> 4 tablespoons grated Parmesan cheese

Place the steaks in a well buttered dish and cover with natural yogourt. Put the finely chopped fennel or celery on the top of each steak. Add salt and pepper. Place the dish in a pre-heated oven Mark 4 350°F for 30–40 minutes, depending on the thickness of the fish. Remove from the oven and sprinkle with cheese. Brown under the grill.

95

Cod with Ginger and Spring Onions

> 4 cod steaks
> 8 tablespoons natural yogourt
> 1 lemon (grate the rind)
> 1-2 tablespoons grated root ginger
> 4 spring onions or 1 tablespoon chopped chives

Place the cod steaks onto a well-buttered dish. Sprinkle with the grated lemon rind and ginger, plus the chopped chives or onions. Add salt and pepper and a little lemon juice. Cover with yogourt. Bake in a pre-heated oven for 30-40 minutes (Mark 4, 350°F).

Oyster Loaves

> This recipe is not for the slimmers or figure-conscious. According to the price, you may use oysters or mussels, or both. This makes a delicious light lunch or supper dish (for six people).

6 brioche rolls or mini cottage loaves or soft bread rolls
$\frac{1}{4}$ lb melted butter
3 dozen oysters or large mussels
Cayenne pepper or tabasco
9 fl oz double cream
$\frac{1}{2}$ pt soured cream
1 lemon
Chopped parsley (optional)

Pre-heat the oven to Mark 4/5 (350°-400°F). Cut the tops off the rolls and scoop out the centres to make six cases. Brush the insides (not forgetting the lids) with the melted butter. Place on a baking-tray and put in a warm oven until crisp; this should take between five and ten minutes. When the rolls are nicely crisp, keep warm until required.

Open the oysters or mussels. If mussels are used, be sure they have been cleaned thoroughly.

Melt 2 oz butter in a pan and add the oysters. Simmer for three to four minutes. Remove the oysters from the pan and add lemon juice and cayenne or tabasco to taste. Reduce the liquid until only a quarter remains. Add both the creams slowly, whisking all the time. Simmer until the sauce thickens (do not boil!). Add the oysters to the sauce for a few minutes so that they are hot. At this point add the parsley if you are using it.

Fill the rolls and serve immediately.

Winter 1982

The Heraldic Deep

An inquiry into the significance of seafood in heraldry, with a special reference, 'that democracy may be preserved,' to the 'socially less fortunate fish.'

Sir George Bellew

Gilbert White or Isaac Newton would perhaps be more at home with the heraldic deep than André Simon. Though they may be interesting enough, there are a lot of somewhat indigestible fish in it.

Yet if we gaze intently we may see swimming about, beyond the mermaids with their mirrors, the tritons blowing conch shells, the dolphins and the sword-fish and the spiky little sea-horses, as delectable an assortment of fish as ever graced an à la carte.

You will see there the noble salmon, the Dover sole, the brown trout, and many another fine fish. They will be *naiant*, or *hauriant*, as the case may be and sometimes *urinant*. *Naiant* of course means just swimming; *hauriant* is upright; and the term with the somewhat indelicate phonetics means head downwards (the reverse of hauriant).

You will see also the lobster, and the crab and some lesser but respected crustacea like the crayfish. And you will see escallops everywhere, for they are the most popular of all the denizens of the heraldic deep.

Of the 'umble cod (though some say he would be the salmon's equal if he weren't so common and if people knew how to cook him) you will catch a fleeting glimpse here and there. I know of one which is

97

borne, appropriately enough, in the coat-of-arms of a family called Codd.

The skate (so undistinguished in name yet an aristocrat au beurre noir) and the hake (so like his name whatever way you cook him), and their rather robust brethren, are rare in heraldry, like sunshine in an English summer.

And absent altogether, so far as I know, will be such horror-comics of the menu card as snoek, monk-fish, saithe and flake, the last three of which, like to masquerade under the nom-de-fish-slab of rock salmon.

The principle governing the use of fish (and indeed all 'charges') in heraldry, is that any sort or kind may be depicted on crest or coat-of-arms, so long as they can be visually identified and, for preference, look decorative too. The system of heraldry is, broadly speaking, a system of marks of identity of decorative kind and having a romantic flavour.

So you see, a salmon would do admirably, because he is fairly distinctive, rather romantic, and very decorative.

But rock salmon! The poor creature has nothing, not even identity; for he only becomes rock salmon when he is skinned and beheaded on account of his repulsive appearance.

Although Britain is an island kingdom set in a silver sea where fish abound, it is, curiously enough to Germany that we have to look for a selection of fish in heraldry which is both more luscious and more imaginative.

No juicier lobster has ever been seen than the one in the coat-of-arms of Von Melem of Frankfurt; *argent a lobster gules*; a scarlet lobster set in a white field. And at the other end of the scale, so to speak, we may note a couple of German post-prandial coats-of-arms, *gules two skeletons of fish in saltire argent*, for Gradel of Bavaria, and *gules the backbone of a fish in bend sinister or*, for Gradner.

The best we can do to match this within our sea-washed shores would seem to be two lobster claws, borne by the family of Tregarthick. Nevertheless two families of Bannyster and Dykes have lobsters for their crests. But they might be unpalatable lobsters, one being gold and the other emerald green.

Crabs are found in some profusion in English heraldry, inelegant though they be. John Gwillim, a seventeenth-century heraldic author of some note, who possessed, and was not shy of committing to paper, a store of miscellaneous information, tells us that 'the Crabs of the Sea are either full and plump or else shear and (after a sort) empty.' Heraldry, like haute cuisine, prefers the former. A crab is the crest of

Danby of Yorkshire and (rather confusingly) the badge of Scrope of Danby; it is borne in the arms of Bridges of Sussex, Crab of Scotland, Bythesea, and others. It is also the crest of Burkin of Colchester who, one would have thought might have preferred an oyster.

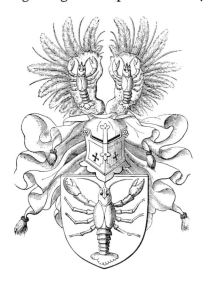

This brings me to confess that I can find no oyster anywhere in heraldry though I have fished for him in many an azure water. An oyster-dredge comes to light, yes, as an ancient badge of a family of Goldringham; but no oyster. Perhaps this is due to that gastronomically noble creature's rather indeterminate and unpreposessing appearance; a shield full of oysters could, I suppose, easily be mistaken for a shield full of quite other things.

Not so the escallop, which I have already mentioned. He has all the visual distinction in the world, with his sharp pointed ears and well defined pattern of ridges. He is unmistakable in a coat-of-arms and a very pretty thing at that.

The escallop shell was the emblem of those who journeyed on a pilgrimage. It was regarded, as indeed it still is in some places, as the visible sign of a pilgrim addressing himself to his meritorious purpose. The origin of this may perhaps be found in the supposition that the tough little shell recommended itself, to those who travelled long distances on foot with minimum equipment, as a convenient cup or dish.

The escallop shell was also the particular device of Saint James of Compostella, one of the twelve apostles, though it was not assigned to him till about 1,100 years after his death. Whether this was done because he had become, long posthumously, the patron saint of pilgrims, or simply because he was originally a fisherman or, indeed, for some other reason, is not known.

To note but one or two cases of the use of escallops, or their shells, in arms is enough. There is, for example, a knight of old, Robert de Scales, '*bel et gent,*' as an ancient poem tells us; he bore '*le ot rouge o cockilles de argent.*' Some might think a salmon more appropriate to his name of Scales. There is another knight of Edward I's time, Nicholas de Villiers who, it is said, returned from his crusade in the Holy Land, with *argent on a cross gules five escallops or*, a red cross on a white field with five gold escallops on the cross.

And there is Sir Anthony Eden, with wheatsheaves and a chevron and three escallops on the chevron.

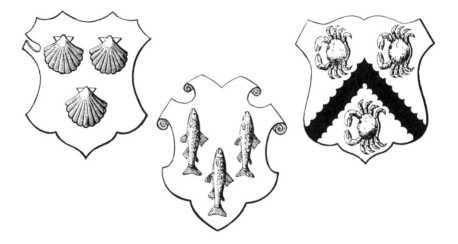

Prawns and shrimps in heraldry are almost, if not entirely, non-existent. Some heraldic works proclaim that the Atsea family have three prawns in their arms; others declare they are not prawns but shrimps. This weighty problem would seem to be settled by the fact that the records of the College of Arms are altogether devoid of Atseas. A picture of the arms of one Dr Atwater, of Henry VIII's time, shows three creatures which might well be prawns or shrimps. Alas it is elsewhere averred that they are crayfish, a not uncommon charge in heraldry.

Even when we turn to the family of Shrimpton, where we might reasonably expect to gather a rich harvest of shrimps, what do we find? Escallop shells.

Although these few thoughts on fishy heraldry were intended to relate to the aristocracy of the heraldic Billingsgate, with perhaps some emphasis on the more noble crustacea, I feel constrained, if only that democracy may be preserved, to say a word about one or two of the socially less fortunate fish. Thus, on a note of kippers, whelks, and eels, I will end.

A kipper *qua* kipper I have not discovered. But the stockfish of Iceland, until recently borne in the arms of the kings of Denmark, stands good proxy. In the Icelandic arms this very dead and decapitated fish, which George Meredith once rather unkindly compared to London, looks every bone a kipper. It is, as a matter of fact, none other than a species of the 'umble cod, split open and dried hard in the air without even a pinch of salt.

As to whelks and eels, the shells of the former decorate the shield of the noble family of Shelley, and eels, alas for the gourmet, sans jelly, and *naiant* very happily, occur in the arms of divers families of that name.

Autumn 1955

When in Season

D.B. Wyndham Lewis

The Scampi (when in season) play
  Round gold Italian shores all day;

The Scampi's girl-friends, for some reason,
  Play with the Scampi (when in season);

Crying '*Ehi!*'[1] and '*Aspettate!*'[2]
  The Fisher speeds to join the party;

And beaming on the final scene,
  Lo and behold La Haute Cuisine!

Fried, floured, breadcrumbed, and at rest,
  With sauce or cheese upon each breast,

Scampi, in all your little eyes
  I spy excitement and surmise;

Your destiny may be, perhaps,
  That of a thousand sterling chaps,

Firm, forthright, fearless, forceful, fond,
  And natural fodder for some blonde[3].

Author's footnotes
  1. 'Hi!' (or 'Oi')
  2. 'Wait a minute!' (or 'Half a mo'!')

Editor's footnote
  3. – or brunette

Summer 1957

A Riviera Dish of Fish

R. Hudson-Smith treads the sun-blessed coast from
Marseilles to Menton in loving quest of its gourmet
fish-dishes from golden bouillabaisse to aromatic loup-de-mer.

It was during lunch Chez Felix, down by the old port of Antibes, that
I found myself eavesdropping shamelessly. It was out of season, so
there were few diners. Graham Greene, immersed in a book, was
rather absent-mindedly eating a dish of grilled red mullet at his
favourite table by the window, and three elderly ladies, also regulars,
were neatly dividing a large loup-de-mer into equal portions.

But it was the conversation at the table next to mine that riveted my
attention. It was between a jolly party of two well-nourished men
with globular outlines and their equally rotund wives who were
tucking in to a huge bowl of that classic fish-stew bouillabaisse,
pausing at intervals to refresh themselves with the excellent rosé wine
of Cassis. In strong Provençal accents they were arguing over the spiny
problem as to whether lobster should be included in a bouillabaisse.

'Mon chèr ami,' one of the men was saying, 'any knave who leaves
lobster out of a bouillabaisse is the sort of fellow who would starve his

children. The mere idea is preposterous!' Nicely put, I thought, all ears. But his adversary was quick with a riposte. 'With great respect, mon vieux, any fool who puts a lobster in that sublime dish would be capable of poisoning wells. It is culinary anarchy. As the great Maître Escoffier said, in preparing food one must always respect its traditional simplicity.' Checkmate.

As the discussion grew more heated – politics and food are two subjects guaranteed to arouse the French – I mentally sided with the purist but on economical rather than gastronomical grounds. As lobsters are wickedly expensive on the Riviera, it seems a needless extravagance to let their delicate flavour drown among the spicy and aromatic ingredients of a bouillabaisse – let alone doubling the price of the dish.

But with or without this costly crustacean, the fish-stew which Curnosky, the Prince of Gastronomes, called 'The Golden Soup' remains the most renowned sea-food on the sun-blessed coast stretching from Marseilles to Menton. Every chef along it has his own idea of what constitutes a real bouillabaisse, but basically the ingredients should be at least six kinds of fish, vegetables, herbs, garlic, oil, and saffron which gives it its characteristically orange colour. The fish are usually whatever Mediterranean denizens the cook can lay his hands on but one is mandatory – *rascasse*, a ferocious-looking rock-fish covered with spikes. Bouillabaisse is a rich and substantial meal in itself, which is just as well for even without lobster it is not exactly cheap and rarely served for less than two persons.

In Marseilles they claim to produce the only veritable bouillabaisse and all others elsewhere are spurious and pale imitations. Admittedly, I have enjoyed some superb ones alfresco on a summer evening at the small restaurants on the Vieux Port, but at the risk of offending the loyal Marseilles gourmets I venture to say that I have sampled others equally as good along the Riviera; restaurants in Nice, St Tropez and Antibes spring to mind.

For the gourmet, chapon, sole, rouget, daurade and loup-de-mer form the quintet of the most delectable Mediterranean fish. Taking them in that order, chapon, though one of the tastiest, is the fish least likely to be found on your bill of fare for it seems to be becoming very scarce. It has an enormous head and white firm flesh and its existence is ignored both in my dictionary and in the 1000 page *Larousse Gastronomique*, so I cannot tell you its name in English. Perhaps it doesn't have one. The soles are usually small but good, though not posessing quite the same delicacy of flavour of the English variety.

Sadly, soles have become so wildly expensive that they have disappeared from the table of many a modest Riviera household – certainly from mine!

The pink rouget (red mullet) are rather small fish with a distinctive and subtle flavour. They are usually served grilled with herbs and without being cleaned out first – a gastronomic detail which led Brillat-Savarin to call them 'the woodcock of the sea'. Daurade (sea bream) is also a highly-esteemed fish and almost certainly on the menu if you are dining in a restaurant of renown. A popular Riviera way of preparing it is grilled with sage.

Completing this somewhat pricey quintet is the loup-de-mer (literally sea-wolf) which is a variety of sea-bass. It is a firm-fleshed white fish and though it lacks a really distinctive flavour, it is a splendid carrier of other aromas.

As a result, the favourite appetite-provoking method of cooking it is on the table before the eyes of the diner, over a little fire of fennel twigs with an occasional dousing of cognac or armagnac to help things along. If the chef is worthy of his toque, he will have stuffed the fish beforehand with a forcemeat containing an assortment of the aromatic herbs so much used in Provençal cooking.

Prepared in this way (au fenouil), it is truly a fish dish to remember, but be warned that the bill may be memorable too.

To keep this item within reasonable bounds, may I suggest that when ordering your loup do not leave the size of the fish to the waiter. Do as the French do and ask to have a selection brought to your table, when you can choose one of suitable proportions; they will be produced without demur. Otherwise, as loup can be pretty big, you may find yourself being served with a monster specimen that the chef has been unable to get rid of. And don't be embarrassed to fix the price after having made your selection for on most menus loup is listed with no price but the laconic initials S.G., standing for *Selon Grosseur* – according to size. Incidentally, the smaller the loup the tastier.

In more modest realms of piscine gastronomy is the ubiquitous friture du pays or friture du golfe. This is a fry-up of small fish, larger than whitebait but smaller than sardines. The locals call them mange-tout for that is how they are eaten, heads, tails, bones and all. Washed down with a chilled regional rosé, a friture makes an appetising starter.

Not to be missed in this category are fresh grilled or fried sardines – one of those rare phenomena on the Riviera, a cheap delicacy. In the picturesque old Place Nationale in Antibes you can sit at a restaurant table in the square and sample the local speciality sardines à l'Antiboise when fresh sardines are rolled in egg and breadcrumbs, fried in oil and served with those trademarks of Provençal cuisine, highly seasoned tomato extract and garlic. It is a dish redolent of the Mediterranean and the south.

You can have no pretensions to being an old Riviera hand unless you have had an Aioli Garni. Every Friday, with the same certainty as a rise in the price of petrol, this traditional dish appears on hundreds of menus in the Alpes-Maritimes. *Ail* is French for garlic and *aioli*, as we have already noted, is mayonnaise mixed with crushed garlic – lashings of it. For an Aioli Garni this unctuous highly-flavoured sauce – sometimes called the butter of Provence – is smeared copiously over a platter of boiled vegetables such as runner-beans, potatoes, carrots and artichokes surrounding a piece of cod.

According to the great chef M Reboul, this dish 'demands a great deal of artistic arrangement', but I haven't noticed any real attention paid to this culinary stricture in my favourite local restaurant. Their Aioli Garni is excellent, nevertheless. it is considered plebian fare, so look for it in modest establishments rather than in de-luxe hotels and

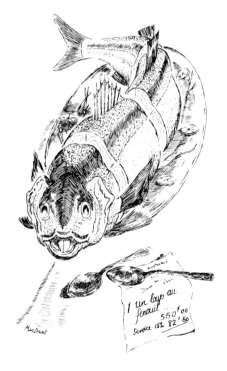

multi-starred temples of gastronomy. If you can't find a place serving an *aioli* in your locality on Fridays then the pastis are on me!

Dr Johnson said, 'The grand object of travelling is to see the Mediterranean.' Agreed, and I hope he enjoyed its fish.

Summer 1983

Cordon Bleu

Carole Walsh

A few packets of Jumbo scampi in the freezer are a very good standby and do not take too long to thaw or cook. For the best flavour take them out of the freezer 2-3 hours before you need them or, if you are not given that amount of notice, put them in a colander and run under cold water for a few minutes. Be sure to dry thoroughly on a kitchen roll before using.

You can also buy Dublin Bay prawns which are sold in boxes of 1.25 kilo and cost around £7 to £8. These are absolutely delicious cut in half and grilled. When cooked, cover with hot garlic butter. This makes a very good hors d'oeuvres or a not too filling main course.

Scampi Mornay

>2 lb large scampi
>2 oz butter
>1½ oz flour
>2 oz grated Parmesan or 4 oz grated Cheddar
>2 egg yolks
>2 tablespoons double cream
>1 small glass sherry (optional)

Blanch the scampi briefly in a court bouillon.

Make a Mornay sauce. Make a roux: add the milk, stirring continuously. Simmer for 5 minutes. Add the grated cheese and the sherry, if you are using it.

Beat the egg yolks and cream just enough to mix them. Take the sauce off the heat. Add the eggs and cream and stir. You may reheat but do not allow to boil. Arrange the scampi in a dish and cover with sauce. Spinach goes particularly well with this dish.

Mushroom Scampi

Another delicious scampi dish is made with mushrooms, rice and garlic.

       2 cups brown or long grain rice
       2 lb scampi
       1 lemon
       $\frac{1}{2}$ lb butter
       1-2 cloves; garlic
       2 tablespoons oil
       1 tablespoon chopped parsley

Cook the rice and keep warm until needed. Dip the scampi in flour. Melt the butter and oil. When hot, add the scampi and the crushed garlic. 3-4 minutes before the scampi is cooked add the sliced mushrooms, salt and pepper and 1 lemon juice to taste. You can add the cooked rice to the scampi and, when very hot, serve with a sprinkling of parsley, or the rice may be served separately.

Marinated Kipper Fillets

A good standby is my mother-in-law's marinated kipper fillets.

You may prepare these with kipper fillets which can be bought in packets. Put them in an air-tight jar and fill with a mixture of corn-oil and lemon juice, and a few whole peppercorns. The quantities should be $\frac{1}{2}$ lemon juice to $\frac{2}{3}$ corn-oil.

Screw the top on very tightly and leave for at least 4 days. Keep the jar in the fridge and they will last as long as your family will allow.

Winter 1982

Meals to Remember

Major-General Sir Hereward Wake

Thirteenth Baron of Clevedon (cr. 1621). Educated at Eton and Royal Military College, Sandhurst. Served in South Africa; wounded once but four times mentioned in dispatches, Queen's Medal, 5 clasps, and DSO. Distinguished service in World War I; ADC to George V; commanded Northants Home Guard in World War II. Freeman of Dover; High Sheriff of Northants; Commander of Légion d'honneur and Order of Crown of Italy. Edited *Swift and Bold.*

The earliest meals of note I can remember naturally took place at my home in Northamptonshire. First, the hunt breakfast when hounds were meeting at the old house and many of the field came in 'booted and spurred', in red coats and black, to attack 'the groaning board'.

109

And, my word, it did groan in those sumptuous days! Besides the hot dishes there was cold ham, tongue, galantine, etc, on the sideboard. I must admit I never saw the 'strong home-brewed ale and good beef' which, according to the old song, was the right breakfast for a foxhunter.

Perhaps I have an even better memory, from those days, of the Christmas-cum-New Year party given annually by the Rector, to which he invited all in the parish who helped in the church – the choir, bellringers, the churchwardens, the sexton and a few special guests for whom room could be found. The good fare provided would be beyond the means of a country parson today. At each end of the long table the Rector and his good lady carved the turkey and roast beef, and helped the sausages and Yorkshire puddings. Then a blazing plum-pudding (made the previous year), followed by mince-pies, home-made cheese and dessert. Crackers produced paper hats – then a novelty. For drinks we had old ale and cider, tea and port wine. Games, songs and dancing to the rattling old rectory piano finished a happy evening, but not before the bellringers had filed out to the church to ring in a happy new year for everyone as the grandfather clock – there was no Big Ben on the wireless – struck twelve.

Then came the South African War, in 1899, to shake us out of our complacency. Meals I remember! Do I *not* remember the endless rule of bully beef and biscuit, biscuit so hard it had to be soaked in water and fried in fat to make it edible.* Tea, sugar and tinned milk we got, but no bread or fresh vegetable for the first six months. For who imagined this war would last longer?

There was the story of the soldier who, revisiting one of his old battle-fields near Ladysmith, two years later, found a ration biscuit he had thrown away – with two of his teeth still sticking in it.

Early in 1901 I had a very different type of experience, no less than lunch at Buckingham Palace with the Prince and Princess of Wales; a meal I certainly remember. Queen Victoria at that time was very ill at Osborne. I had returned home with Lord Roberts, as one of his aides-de-camp, and we drove in procession in State carriages through cheering crowds from Waterloo to the Palace. There was a striking menu, set forth in French, and, of course champagne with which the Prince proposed the Field-Marshal's health in a few well-chosen-words, as the saying is. Lord Roberts made a very brief and courteous

---

* There was still some left in 1940. *Ed.*

reply. A week or so later we rode once more through the streets of London, this time on horse-back, in the great Queen's funeral procession from the Abbey to Paddington Station.

Spring 1956

Meals to Remember

Macdonald Hastings

Educated at Stonyhurst, Macdonald Hastings, son of playwright and author Basil Macdonald Hastings, started his career as a junior PRO for Lyons at Cadby Hall. Prolific, peripatetic broadcaster and journalist, author of the popular Mr Cork series of whodunits, of books of adventure and exploration. Founder-editor of *Country Fair*; war correspondent, game-shot, piscator and paterfamilias.

The order of gustatory battle remains with me now: Colchester Royals, Sole à la Broche garnished with bay leaves and onions; partridges spitted on Toledo swords and served in a flourish of flaming brandy; a savoury of chickens' livers; Tio Pepi, Mersault, Krug, a vintage port and a 100-year-old *fine*.

Trimalchio, when he entertained his guests to a spread of dormice garnished with honey and poppyseed, didn't do it any prouder. I did it on an expense account as a very junior member of the publicity staff of the Trocadero Restaurant.

The next morning I was on the carpet at Cadby Hall. After administering the appropriate rocket, Major Montague Gluckstein dismissed the matter with a comment which he delivered as earnestly as a prayer:

'When you leave this firm, Hastings, I can only express the hope that you will become one of our paying customers; because, God knows, you're the sort of customer we want.'

* * *

The trouble is that, for so much of my life, people have paid me good money to carry out journalistic assignments in places where the best you can expect is the husks of swine. The prodigal intervals, although rewarding, have been brief.

111

I can boast – no, that's not the right verb; at the time I was writing a weekly glamour feature for a woman's magazine called 'A Date with Mac' – I can claim that I have eaten Adriatic scampis (even more succulent, I think, than Dublin Bay's) in the roof restaurant of Danieli's in Venice.

I've chewed Essex natives straight from the dredge with the racing correspondent of *Wheeler's Review*.

I've consumed golden eye from Lake Winnipeg on the giant CPR.

I've had a free meal on Le Tour d'Argent in Paris (which needs a bit of wangling).

I've rejoiced in ribs of beef off a pinewood plate (which flavours the meat deliciously) in the Château Frontenac in Quebec.

I've swallowed a raw shellfish at Positano to the music of a wandering guitarist; and survived them both.

I've attended one of those 'parties of the year' at a fashionable Long Island resort where the bar was guarded by armed cops and where, when I mildly protested that my glass of champagne was flat, was informed, as if I oughtn't to have known better, that all the bottles for the evening's entertainment had been opened already.

I've lived in the logging camps of Vancouver Island where, if the food isn't up to standard, they throw the cook into the river (the consequence is that they can't get cooks unless they pay them about £50 a week).

I've been compelled to consume oriental sweetmeats with a ferret of the Syrian secret police who kept me under house arrest until I capitulated. ('Friend, one sweet; close friend, three sweets.')

I can tell you of the dinner party, while I was still an unbearded youth, when Hilaire Belloc condescended to enquire of me how I bought my burgundy. Ignoring my innocent blushes he gave me the instruction. 'You should do as I do, young man. I always get it in cask.'

I can tell you of my father who loved boiled Spanish onions, with pepper, salt and butter but would only eat them if they were served off a Wedgwood blue plate.

What memorable meals! In the company of men, I can recall only the laughs. In the company of beautiful women, I have never the vaguest recollection of what I have eaten.

Autumn 1959

A Lobster Ballad

John Pudney

How does it feel
To enter the creel
In a solemn hour
In a shallow sea?

How does it feel
To come into power,
To suddenly be
Significant, real?

Nobody cares
How a lobster fares
In the shallow dim
Of the fruitful sea.

Nobody cares
But a bait for him,
Till the hour when he
Royal scarlet wears.

How does it seem
To leave the dream
Of the shallow deep
Of a world of fish?

How does it seem
To fall asleep
In the royal gleam
Of a silver dish?

Autumn 1955

Cordon Bleu

Carole Walsh

Hot or cold, lobsters are a real treat at any time, providing you are not one of those who are allergic to shell-fish. Opinions vary as to the best size for eating. Nowadays people tend to serve a 1 lb lobster per person but I feel there is more meat on a 2 lb lobster. Still, with these things it is a matter of personal preference.

Dressing a Lobster

It is much easier to dress a lobster than a crab. A pointed kitchen knife should be inserted in it in the centre of the hinge between the head and the tail. Then, with the heel of the knife, cut back through the centre of the tail. The line is clearly marked on the shell. It is necessary to remove the green gut which runs down the tail. The rest of the lobster is edible. (This method is for splitting a live or cold fish.)

If the lobster is cold, it only remains to crack the shell on the knuckles and claws. This is done with a short, sharp blow with the heel of the knife – but be sure not to damage the meat inside.

Always make sure when you buy a lobster that the tail is tucked under. If it is not, the lobster is weak and will not have much meat on it when cooked.

Boiling a 2 lb Lobster

Have a saucepan large enough to take the lobster filled with salted boiling water. Plunge the live lobster in and simmer for 15 minutes. Instead of water, a courte bouillon may be used. (Water with sliced onion and carrot, peppercorns and a bouquet garni.)

To really savour the full delicious flavour serve with a light mayonnaise when tepid.

Lobster Thermidor

1 x 2 lb lobster
2 oz butter
1 oz chopped shallots
2 oz roux
½ cup fish or chicken stock
1 tablespoon chopped parsley
2 oz grated Parmesan
1 oz double cream
1 level teaspoon dried English mustard
1 tablespoon dry white wine
salt and pepper

This recipe uses a lobster that has been boiled. Cut the lobster in half and remove both the small bag containing grit and the thin black line running down the tail. Take all the meat from the shell being sure to get the meat from the claws and the knuckles. Cut the meat into pieces about 1 inch square.

Lightly fry the chopped shallots in the melted butter but do not brown them. Add the white wine, the lobster meat, and the fish stock. Simmer for 3-4 minutes stirring all the time. Add some grated cheese, parsley and cream.

Remove from heat, add the dry mustard and mix well. Tip the mixture into the lobster shells leaving some of the sauce in the pan. Add a little butter and the rest of the cheese. Mix well and coat the lobster with it. Glaze under a hot grill until golden brown.

Lobster Newburg

1 x 2 lb lobster
2 oz butter
½ pint double cream
½ pint veloute sauce
2-4 tablespoons brandy

Boil the lobster in the usual way. Remove the meat from the shell and cut into 1 inch pieces. Melt the butter in a saucepan. Add the lobster, salt and pepper and enough brandy to almost cover the lobster. Warm the brandy and flare. Add the veloute and mix well. Simmer for 5 to 6 minutes. When very hot add the cream and just before it boils remove from the heat. Serve on a bed of rice.

Veloute

> 2 oz butter
> 2 oz flour
> ½ pint fish stock
> ½ pint white wine

Make a roux. Add the stock, stirring constantly. Then add the white wine. Bring to the boil and simmer for 30 minutes.

Spring 1983

Pursuit of the Grape

Merlin Minshall

Nobody knows whether Julius Caesar said *Vynum* or *Weenum*. What we do know is that had the immortal Sam Weller been a scholar as well as a classic he would certainly have said: *In winum ... weritas*.

But far more than truth has come into being, thanks to some prehistoric man's chance discovery of how to ferment grape juice: and thereby to raise our forebears above the status of Brute Beast; and enable them to resist illness.

'Wine', says the ancient Babylonian Talmud 'is at the head of all Medicine,' and centuries later, in 595 BC to be exact, the Athenian writer Alcaeus said the same thing.

Together with the invention of how to ferment milk (and so make its life-giving protein transportable) wine made it possible for man to travel long distances and so to explore and discover the world.

Without these two inventions, *homo* would never have become *sapiens*.

Of course Woman may have helped a bit too.

Throughout the ages, wine has inspired much that is great in music, song, literature, painting, philosophy and gastronomy ... together with all those myriad creations of Man that have helped make Woman more nearly divine, and Man himself slightly less bucolic.

'Wine, true begetter of all arts, that be', wrote Hilaire Belloc in his Ode dedicated to another great connoissuer of wine, Duff Cooper.

It is hardly surprising therefore that the pursuit of the Grape has always been one of Man's primary occupations.

John Gay summed it up admirably in the *Beggars' Opera*:
'Women and wine should life employ', and then posed the question:
'is there aught else on earth desirous?' To this many people have
replied 'Money!' but that in itself may be nothing more than the
means and the time to pursue the grape.

Holy Writ is packed with praise of wine:
'Use a little wine ...,' thundered even that arch-puritan St Paul.
'The best wine for my beloved,' whispered Solomon. And he was
named 'the Wise'.
'Drink thy wine with a merry heart,' counsels the Book of Proverbs.
'Wine that maketh glad the heart of man', chants the Psalmist.

Nearer our own times who better summed up the pursuit of the
grape than Calverley in his ageless quip:
Cold water is the best of drinks
The Temperance Party sing,
But who am I, that I should have
The Best ... of anything?

Summer 1962

Tribute to the Oyster

The Detroit Free Press, 12 October, 1899

Let us royster with the oyster — in the shorter days and moister,
That are brought by brown September, with its rouguish final R;
For breakfast or for supper, on the under shell or upper,
Of dishes he's the daisy, and of shell-fish he's the star.
We try him as they fry him, and even as they pie him;
We're partial to him luscious in a roast;
We boil him and broil him, we vinegar-and-oil him,
And O, he is delicious stewed with toast!
We eat him with tomatoes, and the salad with potatoes,
Nor look him o'er with horror when he follows the cold-slaw;
And neither does he fret us if he marches after lettuce
And abreast of cayenne pepper when his majesty is raw.
So welcome with September to the knife and glowing ember,
Juicy darling of our dainties, dispossessor of the clam!
To the oyster, then, a hoister, with him a royal royster
We shall whoop it through the land of heathen jam!

Spring 1984

Cordon Bleu

Carole Walsh

The Sole family is one of our great gifts from the sea. The different ways of cooking it are unlimited, and people who normally will not eat fish enjoy it.

The sole is a flat fish that buries itself under the sand or mud and adapts its colour to its surroundings. In April the sole, which is rather thin at that time, shoots its roe.

The best size to buy if you are serving a whole sole is 14-16 oz. But if you are serving a dish with fillets you can use the bigger sizes which are cheaper and you need to serve only two or three fillets depending on the appetites of your guests.

The simplest and quickest (also, in my opinion, the most delicious) are Sole Pommery and Sole Capri.

Sole Pommery

> 1 sole per person
> 4 oz butter
> 1 dessertspoon oil
> 1 large eating apple
> Juice of half a lemon
> Mango chutney
> Flour
> Salt and pepper

Dip the sole and the sliced apple in the flour. Melt the butter and add the oil. When hot, put in the sole and cook until nicely brown. Add

118

salt and pepper, the lemon juice and the slices of apple two minutes before ths sole is ready. Only touch the apples very gently to turn them or they will break. The exact time for cooking the apples depends on the type used. Put the sole on the dish and decorate with the apples. Place a tablespoonful of chutney on top and sprinkle with chopped parsley.

Sole Capri

This is done in exactly the same way but substituting bananas for the apples.

Sole Veronique

> 1 sole per person or three larger fillets
> The bones of the soles
> 1 carrot
> 1 sliced onion
> The white of two leeks, finely sliced
> A bouquet garni, salt, and black peppercorns
> $\frac{1}{2}$ pint of white wine (preferably Sauterne)
> 2 oz butter
> 2 oz flour
> 8 oz white grapes, preferably muscat
> $\frac{1}{2}$ pint fish stock
> $\frac{1}{4}$ pint double cream

Skin the grapes and remove the pips. Place in a small dish and put it in a bain-marie to heat the grapes.

Make the fish stock. Then make a roux. Add the fish stock and white wine and simmer for 10 minutes. Add salt and pepper and a little sugar to taste. Before serving, remove from the heat and add the cream and the grapes.

Poach the fillets or the whole sole; cover with the sauce and decorate with the rest of the grapes.

If you wish to glaze this dish and you happen to have had some hollandaise over from a previous occasion, add a tablespoonful to the sauce and put under a hot grill for a few seconds.

Sole Portuguaise

> 1 14-16 oz sole per person
> $\frac{1}{2}$ lb large fresh tomatoes or a 1 lb tin of tomatoes
> 1 medium sized shallot (chopped)
> 1 tablespoon chopped parsley
> $\frac{1}{2}$ teaspoon sugar
> salt and pepper

Poach the sole and, while it is cooking, chop the tomatoes. Put a knob of butter in a pan, add the chopped shallot and tomatoes, $\frac{1}{2}$ teaspoonful of sugar, salt and pepper. Cook for 10 minutes. When the sole is cooked, cover with the tomato sauce and sprinkle with chopped parsley.

Autumn 1983

Sorbet

Old Compton's Fancy, November

For his November meal this year, Old Compton has decided to go Chinese. For what will be a light repast, he has chosen two Chinese delicacies – Stirred Scollops and Peking Dust.

Having prepared his scollops in the usual manner, he will cut each into four slices, fry them in lard for one minute, then add shallots, a little salt and slices of fresh ginger. He will meanwhile have dissolved one tablespoon of cornflour in a cup of water. This he will pour over the scollops, stirring all the time. When the sauce turns translucent, this admirable dish is done.

The frozen dust of wintry north China is peculiarly vicious. But it has given rise to a heavenly pudding. Its base is a meringue, topped with a purée of chestnuts, fortified by creamed butter, and flavoured with a little brandy or rum. It is then forced through a sieve so that it covers the base in thin spirals like vermicelli. This miracle is in turn surmounted by whipped cream, garnished with maraschino cherries.

Winter 1969

Meals to Remember

Memories of Food and Wine at Tickerage Mill … on the LNER … and in France, Turkey and Malaya

Lord Kinross

Product of Winchester and Balliol, he was a prolific journalist, wide-ranging traveller, and author of many books from *Society Racket* (1933) through *Portrait of Greece* (1956) to *Morocco* (1971). Mentioned in Dispatches with RAFVR MEF (1940–44) and, later, Press Councillor, British Embassy, Cairo.

Main recreation: cooking. Clubs, not inappropriately, Travellers and Beefsteak.

Meals are more memorable, now that they are cooked by hostesses, than in the days when they were cooked by mere cooks. But there were occasions when the cooks did well enough, all the same. A notable gourmet of this nostalgic period was the late and lamented Richard Wyndham, who was at the same time painter, writer, journalist, country gentleman, traveller, crazy-croquet player, photographer, Don Juan and above all, host. I remember a party he gave one night at the Savoy, in a private ballroom transformed for the occasion into a Sudanese jungle. But I remember especially the delights which emerged from the cellars and the kitchens of his house at Blackboys in Sussex, Tickerage Mill.

Eating and drinking, and such talk as these pursuits might arouse, were the sole objectives of one memorable bachelor week-end, at which the guests were Mr David Tennant, the late Mr A.J.A. Symons, Mr Desmond Flower and myself; the courses at the opening meal were garlic soup, pâté de foie gras flown from Strasbourg, Hamburg cakes each with a poussin inside it, asparagus au gratin and dessert; and the wines were a Mersault and five Château-bottled clarets ranging backwards in time from 1926 to 1874.

This meal was later immortalised by Mr Flower, in terms positively poetic, in the pages of a quarterly devoted to food and wine. Of the Mersault he wrote, 'Like love, it was a dancing thing;' the poussins were 'completely ravishing – if indeed a poussin can ravish.' The wines had various noses – 'a grand nose … an even finer nose … a jocund nose … a slight fault on the nose' – and as to the respective merits of the Pichon Longueville 1899 and the Lafite 1874, there was

disagreement between two camps of guests. 'A third camp,' however, 'which contained a solitary but cheerful guest, declared that they were both grand wines, so what?' The third camp was myself.

I remember a last bottle of that Lafite 1874, on my last visit to Tickerage on leave during the war. My host gave me the precious bottle, which had been brought up from the cellar in mistake for a bottle of port, to drink in the train in the course of a journey up to Scotland, since at that period the restaurant cars were wineless. Proud to think of myself as the only man who had ever drunk Lafite 1874 in a third-class dining coach on the LNER, I savoured the nose and above all relished the taste of half the bottle, at luncheon, then gave it to the waiter to keep for me at dinner. At tea he reassured me, 'Your bottle's all right, sir, I've put it in the fridge for you.' Trying not to show my concern, I rescued it from him; but too late. Despite a desperate attempt to thaw and *chambrer* the princely wine beside the lukewarm pipes beneath the seat of my compartment, it was, as Mr Flower would have put it, 'definitely on the down grade' by dinner time, its 'quiet dignity' for ever impaired.

Since the war I have noticed a distressing tendency among the French to imitate all things English – English sports, English slang, and now ominously English food. The French are beginning to fuss far too much about their livers. A year or so ago I paid a visit to the city of Rheims, as one among a number of guests invited to celebrate, with a series of services and banquets and bacchanalia in general, the unveiling of a window in the cathedral to the honour and glory of champagne.

One morning – it was the eve of the Feast of St Remigius – we were led for an hour or so over some of the eighteen miles of champagne cellars of Möet et Chandon at Epernay, then were driven in cars, by Princes of Champagne dressed as English sportsmen, to the vineyards of Lanson Père et Fils at Verzenay. By this time we were both thirsty and hungry. Our thirst was soon quenched with goblets of Lanson Père et Fils – except for that of Mr Graham Greene, who asked for, but could not obtain a whisky and soda. Luncheon, however, was not quite ready. My neighbour at table. Mr Evelyn Waugh, hungrily picked up the menu. I observed his face grow suddenly flushed and his eyes grow white – always a signal of danger, as I know from experience, with this novelist. I myself picked up the menu and saw why. It read: '*Potée Champenoise; Salade; Fromages; Fruits.*

Soup, salad, cheese and fruit – was this a meal to lay before a party of Englishmen, hungry for the lavish products of the French cuisine after a five mile walk through cellars? Mr Waugh and I, and an Irish neighbour, Lord Wicklow, fell into an earnest conclave together. Would it be etiquette for us, we asked one another, to ask for second helpings of soup? Oliver Twistlike we did so, and got them. Then, to our discomfiture, the pangs of hunger already thus half assuaged, huge dishes of meats were placed before us. Potée Champenoise, it became evident, was a dish in two instalments: first the soup, then the meat which had been stewed in it. We over-ate with relief, suffering afterwards, to our faint disappointment, not a twinge of sweet French heartburn. For champagne stew is as much wholesome schoolroom fare as Irish.

Probably the best cooking outside France is that of Turkey. Here, in a restaurant, you go straight to the kitchen, and take your pick from an array of succulent dishes, steaming on the hob. There are *dolmas* — marrows, tomatoes, peppers and vine-leaves, stuffed with minced meat, rice, herbs and pine kernels. There are egg-plants cooked in dozens of ways, of which the richest is the *Imam Bayildi* — so called because the Imam fainted at the expense of the oil used in its cooking. There are *köfte*, meat rissoles, of which the fattest and most succulent are the *Kadin Budu*, called after a woman's thighs. After several weeks of this sort of fare I lived for several more weeks on nothing but yoghurt, a meal in itself — of a kind.

Probably the worst food outside France is in Greece, and the worst in Greece is in the monasteries of Mount Athos. Here you start the eating day after church at 9.30 a.m. with dried cod and a kind of porridge, washed down by vin rosé, and finish it before church at 5.30 p.m., with dried cod and a kind of porridge, washed down by vin rosé. If you are lucky you may get a dish of ink fish, cooked in its own ink; if you are unlucky — as in the Russian monastery — you may get vinegar instead of vin rosé.

Outside Europe the most memorable foods I have eaten are the rice dishes of Persia, light as cumulus clouds, and the ducks of Malaya, impaled and cooked on spits of sugar-cane. In Malaya too I have tasted the delicate heart of a coconut palm — perhaps the most expensive dish in the world. The planter in whose house I ate it ordered his servants to go out in the middle of dinner and cut down a whole coconut tree, that I might taste it.

In Sumatra I missed by one day the notorious local *Reistapfel* — a rice dish garnished with about a hundred spiced side dishes.

'If only you could stay over Thursday!' my Dutch hosts bemoaned.

'That is our half-holiday, and then we have the *Reistapfel*. First we change into our swimming trunks. Then for an hour or so we drink gin' – the record consumption, I afterwards learnt, was that of a Dutch archaeologist who downed 106 gins before dinner – 'Then, for another hour or so we eat the *Reistapfel*, and we drink the beer, and when we become too hot we go.out into the garden, and our servants turn the hose on us, and then we come back and eat more *Reistapfel* and drink more beer, and after an hour or so more we fall asleep and our servants carry us home.'

It is perhaps just as well that I was never in Sumatra on a Thursday.

Summer 1957

The Missing Sorbet

A Nostalgic Enquiry

John Bygott

Sandwiched between 'Somersetshire Pudding' and 'sore throat' in the analytical index of Mrs Beeton's *Book of Household Management* are to be found the recipes for Sorbets. Cream Sorbets, Gooseberry with Maraschino Sorbet, Grape, Lemon, Noyeau and Strawberry Sorbet. In the text there is even a picture – rather a bad one – of the Grape Sorbet looking sadly like a fruit and ice cream mixture which has begun to reach melting point and, at that temperature, has been emptied into a wine glass. But in more modern cookery books there is complete silence on the subject of the sorbet. Once an integral part of a complete meal, it has vanished as though it had never existed.

The *Dictionary of Gastronomy* defines the sorbet as 'A small water-ice flavoured with wine and liqueurs and served halfway through elaborate meals of many courses.' The *Oxford Dictionary* makes somewhat heavy weather of its derivation [ad. Turk. shorbet (see sherbet) perh. influenced by It. Sorbire, to imbibe), but goes on to give some entertaining early references to the word:

1858 – Washington tr Nicholay's Voy III.X 'of the beurage which they do cal Sorbet, they do much use to drink in the Summer.'

1766 – Smollett. Trav XIX 1 308. 'Among the refreshments of these warm countries, I ought not to forget mentioning the Sorbettes.'

By the mid-nineteenth century we appear to have moved away from the sherbet simpliciter and arrived at the sorbet complexiter or ice cream sweet.

1864 – *Daily Telegraph* Sept 27. 'The menu ... meandered gracefully through fish, fowl and truffles and finally melted away into sorbets.

1885 – Mabel Collins – Prettiest Woman v 'The sorbets are delicious sweets of almonds, pistachio, chocolate or coffee.'

Somewhere, therefore, between 1766 and 1864 the Sorbet proper must have come into its own, and it continued in popularity, certainly at formal dinner parties, into the 1930s.

Escoffier (1846 to 1935) writes, 'Sherbets and their derivative preparations consist of very light and barely congealed ices, served after the entrées. They serve in freshening the stomach; preparing it to receive the roast. They are, at once, appetisers and helps to digestion.' He goes on to point out that they (he uses here the word sherbet which with happy insouciance he alternates with sorbet) may be prepared from the juices of every fruit and from every wine and liqueur. He describes one – Sorbet à la Sicilienne which is far nearer iced water-melon laced with maraschino than it is like any ice.

As already mentioned, the derivation of the word sorbet is not easy to trace. It is clearly connected with the Latin word *sorbitio*, a drink (from sorbeo, to sup, swallow, etc.), but its close connection with sherbet is more difficult to explain. The word sherbet has been long associated in the east with cool fizzy drinks and is itself an eastern word. Sherbet possesses the right sort of sedative properties with which to soothe the oriental stomach regularly inflamed with the fiercest *capsicum frutescens* – or chilli sauce – and probably the first sorbets were, in fact, sherbets served in the role of sedlitz powders in between the two services of the immense gorgean meals. As the vigorous influence of the New World made itself felt, the emphasis must have moved away from the sibilation of the sherbet and towards the more solid properties of the water-ice. This is pure surmise but it is clear that the American influence is present. There is a variety of sorbet actually called a 'spoom'!

And now the sorbet is replaced with Alka-Seltzer. The gentle regurgitations induced by the sherbet potion have given way to the bicarbonate of soda 'burp', and we have not gained in the exchange. Traditionalists may shed tears over the missing sorbet – but to do so is but to mistake effect for cause. It is not the passing of the sorbet that is to be regretted so much as the reason for its demise, namely the restriction of modern purses and stomachs – not to say leisure – which has eliminated its *raison d'être*.

To this extent, therefore, my title is misleading. The sorbet is not missing in the sense that it is mislaid or waiting to be found, like some edible sleeping beauty, and revived by the gourmet's kiss to take its ancient place in the course of the meal.

That, alas, can never happen. No magic can restore to us the lost age of elegant dining. But it is missing in the sense that it is forgotten – laid aside in a corner in order to make more room for modern life to rush heedlessly by. Surely such a tried and trusted friend should not be discarded in favour of a pill? In the home of any true gourmet there should be found – not a bottle of bisurated magnesia – but at least two recipes for sorbets with instructions to take one after every heavy meal

or, in exceptionally severe and fortunate cases, between the entrée and the roast.

*   *   *

And here is one recipe from *Chef Patissier* G. Bianchi of *The Ivy*:

> Boil 6 oz sugar with 1½ pints water and the rind of 2 lemons. Add the juice of 2 lemons and 2 oranges. Allow to cool. When cool add ½-pint Champagne. Strain and freeze (in a *Sorbétière*). When nearly frozen add a well beaten white of egg.
>
> *Autumn 1957*

Miss Vino

Women are most beautiful in Autumn; they have the summer inside them

William Younger

Wine is a male thing. That's the view and it's backed by enough tradition to make argument on the matter a short, red carpet to a next-day duel. A more impulsive reaction has sometimes been observed: in ancient Rome Egnatius Maetennus beat his wife to death for drinking out of the vat, but this of course may have been due to thrift and not to temper. In milder ways his view has prevailed and there is no Goddess of Wine. I have never quite understood why.

It may be because women do not make wine. (I know one who does and magnificent it is.) In the low, grey tanks of the Douro no woman goes to tread the grapes. In barns and outhouses of Burgundy, Granny

131

may shout comments from the kitchen door, but it's the men who tend the wooden tubs bubbling with fermentation. The cool cellars smelling of stone are man's territory – an expert kingdom of male moles.

These reflections are provoked by autumn. Women are most beautiful in autumn. They have the summer inside them. In spring they are like the first leaves on the vine, bright and exciting with promise but pale because they are only beginning to show themselves to the sun. In autumn they have the warmth and assurance of the grapes: some, like those in Alsace, glowing with a gold light under the skin: others with a dark vitality made vivid by the bright air of September.

Yet no wine goddess. Why not? The prototype is there in those girls with cornucopias who pour torrents of stone fruit salad into the fountains of rococo Europe. But which of these cornucopias is filled only with grapes and which of them is directed into an elegant marble vat? A select and isolated few. For the most part the wind which flutters their draperies is that which idles among clusters of the Pinot Blanc Chardonnay.

Autumn is the time *par excellence* for tasting wine. There is a clearness in the air – the hint of frost – which provokes a clarity of the palate. (Brilliance is, in this context, the accurate word.) It is a time for drinking the delicate wines: dry Muscadets from the Loire: Lutomer Riesling from Yugoslavia: light, cool, flowery wines from the Middle Moselle – Berncastel, Graach, Uerzig, Wehlen, and Zeltingen, some with a bouquet like a spring day which, paradoxically, fits them so much better for drinking in the autumn than in the spring: above all, a time for sherry, the dry, pale-coloured finos some of which have the finest flower-bouquet of any wine I know, and the Manzanillas with the freshness in them of the sea breeze which sometimes cools the 'Manzanilla town' of Sanlucar de Barrameda at the mouth of the Guadalquivir. Sherry is, alas, seldom drunk in large enough glasses in this country. In France I have been given it before dinner in claret glasses, filled almost to the brim, which I regard as a civilised method of dealing with the matter. Sherry is not a wine to be fiddled with. It is a wine, and a great wine at that; and it can, and should, be drunk with more foods than people now fit to it.

The idea that women can't, or don't, or won't taste wine is dying the death which it deserves. The fact that it remains alive at all is partly due to women themselves. They will tell you immediately what they feel about a scent but not what they think about a wine. They either become shy, fearing to look foolish, or tactful, allowing their escort to be the Sole Arbiter. (This is not a pun on Wheeler's menu but I commend the name to the chef.) In general, of course, men have the greater interest in wine and take the greater delight in the expertise of

wine drinking. As they are – again in general – the greatest gourmets and the greatest cooks, so they will always be the greatest tasters. But if one has a good bottle to share and a happy woman to share it with, and if she has enough of the gift of quietness to be able to taste in silence as wine must be tasted, then one will hear sensible things.

Sometimes her silence will be one of dismay. She will be struck dumb by the thought that she cannot speak wine-language. She may listen to the talk of connoisseurs as a stranger might listen to a tribal incantation: *goût de terrôir, corsé, sève, pelure d'oignon*. She may be confused by an apparent preoccupation with a peculiar form of hunting: *oeil de perdrix, queue de renard, queue de paon*. Or she may be diverted by the Hogarthian picture of a Riesling 'nose'. But she will surely recognise those words which touch her more closely: *robe, tendre, velouté*, and the Burgundian description of wine *qui a de l'amour*.

Set before her a Bouzy Rouge from Champagne and a Volnay from Burgundy. Let her compare the two: the crisp, red wine from the Marne with its savour of burgundy, cool and mellow (and four or five years old if possible): and the greater, more delicately-rich wine from Volnay. She will quickly find both the likeness and the difference and will tell you so in feminine terms as descriptive as many in the male vocabulary. There are, after all, not a few feminine wines, even among the clarets of the Médoc: Gruard-Larose and sometimes Rausan-Ségla, for example.

And one should not be rude to them. Heating them (the wines) indelicately before a fire is not a treatment to which they respond with gratitude. Claret is drunk much colder in the Médoc than it is in this country where to *chambrer* a wine has become an addiction rather than a technique. One sympathises with the waiter when a young man tastes his wine and sends the bottle back for 're-heat'. What else is there to do but put it through the turkish bath process? Back it comes, not quite but nearly steaming. The wine is insulted, the waiter resigned, and honour is satisfied. Youth will be served.

And why not liken wines to women or, for that matter, women to wines? Which of the wines can be visualised as that gay girl whose mouth, so Chaucer said, was as sweet as honey or apples? How do you envisage Miss Pouilly-Fumé? As an ash-blonde with slanting eyes? What about Miss Flor de Jeréz? The possibilities of competition are extensive and this type of contest is popular. I remember a few years ago in the West Indies a close race for the beauty prize between, among others, Miss Sanitary Laundry and Miss Calor Gas Factory. (Both girls were remarkably pretty.) Let us vino drinkers select our Vino Queens. Miss Bouzy Rouge – (in some quarters the title might be open to misunderstanding)? Miss Botrytis Ginerea, which sounds more bewitching perhaps than Miss Pourriture Noble? Miss Sleepy Berry as an alternative contender from the Rhineland? Or should we give the prize to a more homely and more constant companion, one with occasional temper but more frequent cheerfulness, a country girl with a happy body, Miss Vin de Pays or Miss Vino de la Tierra?

* * *

A brief glossary of wine terminology employed earlier in his article.

Gôut de terrôir	– A taste distinctive of the soil of the vineyard.
Corsé	– Full-bodied.
Sève	– The inner taste, or heart, of the wine.
Pelure d'oignon	– A brown tint in some wine (Hermitage, for example).
Oeil de perdrix	– Of white wine with a pink tint.
Queue de renard	– The taste of some old wine which has been affected by the decay of the lees.
Queue de paon	– The taste of a bland, charming wine.
Robe	– Deep, red colour in a wine.
Tendre	– A soft wine.
Velouté	– Velvety.
Qui a de l'amour	– (Burgundy.) Used of great wine with vigour and bouquet.

Autumn 1958

Lean Times Ahead

Michael Watkins

It may be of less than conspicuous interest to you, but recently I celebrated my 18,250th day on this planet. Very likely you take these casual anniversaries in your stride. I, on the other hand, find it rather humbling that I have been around so long without being blown to smithereens in the duty-free shop at Heathrow Airport, without engaging in the undignified practice of jogging, or being obliged to eat in motorway cafés. In these respects, and others, I have been spared.

Not to put too fine a point on it, I am exceedingly grateful still to be here, breathing in and breathing out on such a regular basis. Environmentalists denigrate the quality of the stuff that fills our lungs; to me it feels just great. So far I have avoided beriberi, gout, spondylarthritis and many other afflictions which make people so irritable in the morning. But to tell you the absolute truth I had been feeling a trifle off-colour since the episode of the Orient Express.

Perhaps I'd better clarify that. In my role of travel-writer I have contracted to do a series for that inestimable journal *The Times* (which God preserve! Advert.) on 'Great Destinations of the Past'. You know: Monte Carlo, Baden Baden, Valley of the Kings; and, of course, Venice via the Orient Express. Which is really a gas, if you'll forgive the Americanism. Champagne, caviar, feather boas, white fedoras, tortoiseshell cigarette holders all the way. And you know how gassy even the best champagne can be. When I arrived at Santa Lucia station on the Grand Canal, the Hotel Cipriani speed-boat whisked me across the lagoon and I was reminded, inconsequentially, of Robert Benchley's newspaper assignment to Venice and of the cable he sent his editor: *Streets full of water stop please advise.*

Anyway, after the gastronomic overdoses of the Express and Cipriani's, I returned to Needham Market replete. Yes, you could say that: replete. So I crossed our bosky Suffolk valley of the Gipping to take a three days' crash course at Shrubland Hall Health Clinic, the 1740 mansion, home of Lord and Lady de Saumarez. The grounds and terraces, described in *Country Life* as 'perhaps the most spectacular of English classical gardens', were laid out by Sir James Barry in the style of the Villa d'Este, outside Rome. Not that this has the slighest bearing on my 'cure'.

Which went something like this: arrive at 4 p.m. on Sunday, shown to room six by butler type person. Open window to see, across valley, shadowy outline of my own Tudor pile; much reassured by thought that I'd be able to telephone complaints if anyone left lights on all night. Unpack dressing gown, track suit, four lurid paperbacks, *Oxford Book of Quotations* (which I take everywhere) and bar of Cadbury's Fruit and Nut chocolate, which I hide behind vase. At 4.30, wearing dressing gown, have consultation with Sister; she wants to know that I'm 18,250 days old, that I'm a writer, that I have no pet allergies. She takes my blood pressure, which is a small scientific miracle, so normal is it. Height 5'11", weight 11st. 3lbs., waist 33 inches (less if I suck in the equatorial wobble).

At 5.30 is my consultation with Lady de Saumarez, herself a stunning example of the tenets she holds for a healthy constitution. It would be unchivalrous to disclose her age; be satisfied that she looks ten years less. She tells me that more patients suffer from stress — treadmill stress or the domestic variety — than from obesity (although she has had two who, on medical advice, had to lose ten stones). Some come to stop smoking. Others to recuperate from a bereavement or broken marriage. Some, of course, to lose weight by diet or fasting. Why can't we do it at home and save all that money, I ask. Have you tried, she replies. Fair enough: just you try living off half a dozen orange segments a day when the rest of the family is wolfing up the veal cordon bleu. It's extremely hard to be a closet health addict.

Supper is served at 6 p.m. Lady de Saumarez has decided that a light fruit diet would do me no harm, so I collect tray bearing one pear and five grapes. Meet woman High Court judge who gives favourable verdict on small bowl of yoghurt. Also meet attractive German girl who is trying to give impression that she's enjoying cup of hot water with slice of lemon drifting on surface. Try to persuade German girl to inspect Villa d'Este gardens with me, but she says she couldn't make the 100 steps down there. I retreat to room six with *Oxford Book of Quotations* for company. Sleep erratically, dream of Welsh rarebits and German girls.

Woken at 7.20 a.m. with breakfast tray: cup of hot water and lemon, four or five grapefruit segments, and chit listing treatments — massage at 8.30, sauna at 11.30, appointment with Dr Haigh at 10 a.m. Treatments given in the dungeons. Very suitable. Massage pure torture, sauna not much better — from Sahara heat, plunge into icy pool, repeat three times each in space of half an hour, rubbed down with salt, assaulted by icy jet of hosed water. Oh yes, very jolly. Dr

Haigh gives thorough examination, concludes warily that I'm not bad for a 18,250-day-old.

By which time it's lunch at midday. Never have I taken so long to devour a slice of melon, each drop of juice counts. Listen to Norwegian woman tell me about her weight problem, listen to Essex farmer's wife tell me about her last operation. Can see my cure's going to be delirious fun. Draw covert of library, drawing room and corridors, but German girl has gone to earth. Swim a few lengths of the outdoor pool, do a few press-ups in gymnasium. Feel simply ghastly.

After dinner (self-served at 6 p.m., half an orange and slice of pineapple, eaten in the conservatory – takes huge restraint not to molest rare African orchids) I try to join in the spirit of the thing, but everyone is either playing bridge, watching cookery programme on telly or talking about their favourite restaurants. Wheeler's, incidentally, comes fairly well out of that. German girl still missing; probably died of malnutrition. Retire to room; rather concerned for chocolate bar's safety – can't trust any one these days. Transfer it from behind vase to under bed. Sleep deeply, dreamlessly.

Tuesday. Feel absolutely marvellous. Head clear, eyes shining, tobacco craving gone. Leap down stairs two at a time to swim thirty lengths before breakfasting off the most delicious mushy sort of stuff I've ever tasted – though, unaccountably, cannot manage it all. Meet German girl in pool. Think she rather admires my physique, since she agrees to come for walk around estate with me between her kneip water therapy and colonic irrigation. At 9.30 have underwater massage (head above water, of course) before walk with new German friend. Intended to be short walk but we get lost, so turns out to be long walk. Loads of sheep everywhere, all munching far too much grass. Saw Norwegian woman smoking behind a bush. German girl has lovely complexion: probably all that hot water and lemon. Time for my steam cabinet then, a very sweaty business and not all that much of a laugh because I get a frightful nose itch that I can't do anything about because my hands are inside the contraption and my nose is outside.

Bit of luck at lunch. Cannot manage my last three orange segments, so donate them to German girl. Could have got £1 a segment from anyone else on the black-market. Have another swim together, then play Scrabble all afternoon. I allow her to beat me since I feel it might give her a little more self-confidence. We are invited by partisan group to make evening recce to Sorrel Horse pub at front of drive, but we're too goody-goody and say 'No, thanks!'

We dine romantically off an apple, six grapes and a cup of warm water. Stomach rumblings have quite subsided. We tell each other how fit we look and how we can't understand why people 'out there' can drink dry Martini, eat steak and chips and treacle tart and eggs and bacon and jam roly-poly and then we smile bravely at each other and say it's not for much longer. We part lingeringly at 7.30 p.m. for bed.

Places like Shrubland Hall may sound as if they are designed for the pampered privileged; but this is not completely accurate. The rich go, of course, but so do hairdressers, airline stewardesses, exhausted Fleet Street editors, jaded housewives, resting actors. It takes, as they say, all sorts. Health is also the great leveller; in addition to which it's virtually impossible to be patronising when you're in a dressing gown or stretched naked on a masseur's table. There's not much need for a tiara at Shrubland. I dare to say that a shopgirl and a duchess would get on pretty well together sweating it out in the sauna. Class becomes an irrelevance when you're having colonic irrigation.

But I'm on my way. Final swim, forty lengths today. Final sauna and icy plunges. Then a sitz bath: your bottom in hot water, your feet in a bowl of cold water. Vice versa, and so on. Good for circulation, but glad friends can't see me. Wonderful salad lunch before appointment with Sister, to get my 'certificate': like Speech Day at school. I've lost 3 lbs. in weight and two inches around the waist. Still 5'11'' in height. German girl slightly tearful at my departure, but I buck her up by telling her she has shredded carrots to look forward to for dinner.

Oh yes, if any future incumbent of room six is interested, there's still a bar of Cadbury's Fruit & Nut under the bed.

Winter 1983

A Wine By Any Other Name

Leonard Bernstein

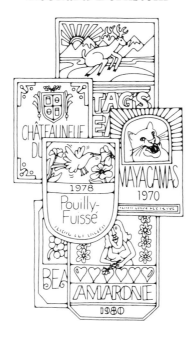

A bunch of us black-belt wine-snobs were sitting around at dinner discussing some of the urgent social matters of the hour, like whether or not the '61 Latour was ready to drink — a conversation, which among wine snobs, could last three days. The waiter arrived, and Reginald, our guiding spirit, ordered a Châteauneuf-du-Pape with mignonettes of lamb bordelaise. We turned to him aghast.

'Surely, Reginald, a red Bordeaux would be more compatible', someone said.

'Possibly a Clos de Vougeot, or any good red Burgundy would be more subtle.'

'Perhaps even a Rhine', I said, straining to appear both daring and sophisticated. '*Why* are you ordering a Châteauneuf-du-Pape?'

'Because I like the way it *sounds*,' said Reginald.

Indeed, it has been said of Châteauneuf-du-Pape that more bottles have been ordered because of the name than because of the wine. It may also be true of Pouilly-Fuissé and Beaujolais; there's something elegant about rolling those delightful sounds off the tongue.

And so, while there is much talk about the character of wine – the nose, the balance, the colour – there is an underworld argument that says wine is ordered because of its name. Wine snobs fear to admit it, but privately concede that they prefer the sound of a snappy Puilly-Fuissé to a cumbersome and plodding Muscadet.

Therefore the time has come to confess this secret failing of connoisseurs and to list the five great wine names.

It would be difficult to steal top honours from **Châteauneuf-du-Pape** although there is some disparity between the quality of the name and the quality of the wine. It's not that the wine is bad; it's perfectly sound, hearty Rhône Valley wine, excellent with beef stew or game. But it is no better than ordinary in the wine hierarchy, surpassed by so many red Burgundies, red Bordeaux and Spanish Riojas. But ah, the name. Nothing surpasses the curious poetry and peculiarity of Châteauneuf-du-Pape.

Pouilly-Fuissé is second – a charming, flutelike sound, like the flight of a hummingbird or a quickly stolen kiss. It is delicacy and melody combined, and the absolutely perfect wine for a young man to order on his first date with a lovely and impressionable woman. And after the impression the wine stands up: a dry and fruity white Burgundy. Indeed, where can you get good wine and a solo on the flute all at the same time?

Mayacamas – the curious throaty sound of the viola – is difficult at first to love. It sounds like an Inca emperor, but is in fact an Indian word meaning 'howl of the mountain lion'. On this alone it is worth ordering because someone at the table is certain to ask what it means.

Mayacamas is one of California's premium wineries, bottling an excellent Chardonnay as well as first-rate Cabernet Sauvignon and Zinfandel. The name has a certain pied beauty which transcends curiosity; it has marvellous resonance, mystery and a haunting melody.

Amarone is one of the great Italian red wines, a wine of incredible depth, bouquet and breed. Forget about that, however, and listen to the name – preferably pronounced by Luciano Pavarotti – Am-mahr-roh-nay; a siren song, a seduction.

There was once a young man hopelessly in love, and yet the love was not shared. So he took her to a secluded Italian restaurant, in a quiet corner, and ordered Amarone. It was seven pounds – more than he could afford – but his heart was past such considerations. He pronounced it perfectly – Amarone – and the waiter stood at attention, raised his eyebrows, and repeated it. 'I think we have only one bottle left', he said. The wine was velvet. And the sound? It was like Heifetz playing Schubert, and their hearts were joined forever.

Stag's Leap – and here comes an argument. How could I – you are thinking – follow Amarone with Stag's Leap; the strings with percussion? Well, an orchestra is many sounds, and one of the good sounds – one of the great names – is Stag's Leap. Another of the small, premium California wineries, Stag's Leap is prized for its Petite Sirah as well as its Chardonnay. More important, it has this bizarre, muscular name that conjures up memories of Teddy Roosevelt attacking at San Juan Hill.

Perhaps at one time this might have been a trifle too combative to qualify as a great wine name, but we have had enough melody and enough curiosity, and what we need is a bit of Americana to celebrate the emergence of California wines. Don't think you have to study wine snobbery at the Sorbonne. They give a good course in the Napa Valley. Today, snobbery is international.

What a pity that wineries bottling excellent wine have no sense of the drama or the elegance of the name. Perfume companies name their products Chanel or Réplique; wineries are named Schramsberg and Gallo.

Don't expect Reginald to admit it, but here are the three names that dedicated wine snobs ignore.

Some of the worst names make the best wines, and **Muscadet** leads the list. The name has no majesty, a perfectly common union of sounds and syllables that really belongs on a can of beer. The wine, however, is lovely, a fruity, semi-dry wine from the Loire Valley. It is almost always the best value on the restaurant's wine list. That's because nobody wants to say Muscadet when they can say Pouilly-Fuissé for only a few pounds more a bottle.

Schloss Vollrads. It seems unfair to include the German wines on the list of the three worst names, the language being so guttural, but then a bad name is a bad name. In fairness to the Germans I am limiting the list to one classic example. Others might reasonably argue that Germany could run away with all three places.

I don't think I need dwell on why Schloss Vollrads is a terrible name for a wine or almost anything else. There it is, right in front of you, like a locomotive puffing and steaming into the Berlin station.

Gewürztraminer. If you wanted to open a sausage shop – hang giant liverwursts and salamis right in the window – a terrific name for the shop would be Gewürztraminer. It has that husky, Polish/Hungarian melody; that sausage, hot mustard and sauerkraut flavour. Indeed, if the Alsatians (whose wine this is) had not named their national sauerkraut-and-sausage dish choucroute, they might have used Gewürztraminer. It's just right – but it's all wrong for a wine. The wine is a spicy, flowery white from the eastern border of France and it deserved a better name. A pity. Third place to Gewürztraminer.

So there are the three worst – clumsy, plodding, gutteral names – that sound simply awful in the company of fine crystal and silver. Which wine snob, I ask you, will order a Schloss Vollrads – a sound likened to a tyre going flat – when he could have an Amarone and a thousand violins?*

* * *

At a recent tasting of the wines of Château Lafite-Rothschild, including all the great vintages from 1945 to the present, Eric de Rothschild was asked about his favourite vintage. 'The '59', he answered, 'if you like young wine.'

---

* Extracted from *The Official Guide to Wine Snobbery*, published by Elm Tree Books (© *Leonard Bernstein*)

Spring 1984

Scholars' Joy

Anthony Lejeune

The genial Mr Gilbert Harding recently expressed his sympathy with 'the dreadful dietary customs' of the post-war generation, and went to Cambridge to provide a party of starving undergraduates with at least one good lunch.

Certainly, young men with a taste for good living find themselves in a hostile world of canteens, artificial cream and tins of luncheon meat. They are oppressed by taxation, the Catering Wages Act and the prevailing idea that the word 'servant' is a term of abuse. At one expensive Oxford restaurant the customers have to translate the menu to the waiters, except for the first item, which is readily understandable – 'Soupe'.

As Marshal Foch said, 'My cen⁺re is broken: my flanks are turned: I attack.' In spite of everything, there is a great revival in the arts of the table. Young people talk knowledgeably about wine and even manage to drink it. There are libraries of good books which forbid them to be wine-snobs and an even more influential cartoon by James Thurber. ('This is a naive domestic burgundy with almost no breeding, but I think you will be amused by its presumption.') New food and wine societies flourish in both Oxford and Cambridge, and there is a Varsity match for blindfold wine-tasting, although it does not yet entitle the participants to a half cordon bleu. Wine merchants gladly send lecturers and samples. Oxford has even enjoyed a lavish beer and cheese tasting, opened by Philip Harben and conducted by Donald McCullough.

The vagaries of taxation have brought light wines to high tables where once the great vintages reigned in exclusive splendour; but champagne still holds chief place in the ceremonial life of the University – flowing freely at commemoration balls, towed behind a punt on May morning, mixed with stout at bump suppers, drunk gratefully on the steps of the examination schools.

A survey of the universities of the world at dinner would be instructive but austere. Most American colleges are 'dry', and even a football dinner is apt to stay itself with flagons of milk. A club dinner in Bangkok is usually washed down with rice-spirit and soda water. The German student drinks with his Corps at a favourite beer-garden;

the French boy learns about wine at his father's table. But only the English undergraduate knows the solemn joy of dressing up in 'soup-and-fish' for the high ritual of a formal dinner undisturbed by the frivolous presence of ladies.

Dr Johnson said that only once in his life had he refused an invitation to dinner in order to work, and then he did nothing. This very human story has been approved by most of our learned institutions. In what other country could it be a necessary condition for becoming a lawyer that the student should have eaten at least seventy-two dinners in the hall of what is still called his Inn? It used to be said of an eminent Lord Chief Justice that port was the only thing he judged well. The significant point is that His Lordship was rather flattered.

Cambridge boasts a Shakespeare Society which once a term heroically tackles a nine-course breakfast; but it is at Oxford that the dinner really comes into its own. There you will find dozens of dining clubs and hundreds of societies which hold at least an annual dinner. (Many of them hold it three times a year – the Academic Annual Dinner, the Calendar Annual Dinner and the Farewell Annual Dinner.) Sometimes the members wear coloured facings on their dinner jackets and practise ancient customs, such as betting on the number of beads in a glass or sconcing the youngest member in champagne. They will probably dine in a panelled room, illuminated by candles in silver candlesticks, waited on by college servants. Their dining committee will have chosen the menu after much discussion, encouraged the chef, selected and perhaps even imported the wine.

If they are high-spirited and of an enquiring turn of mind, they may make some odd experiments, which after all is the way to learn. Because there are no overheads, they do get value for the money they spend. One society recently worked through oysters, caviare, asparagus and frogs' legs before the serious eating began. Another made a triumphal progress through smoked trout, artichoke soup, salmon steaks, champagne sorbet, roast duck with three kinds of salad, pineapple in kirsch, and caviare. The seventy guests used 491 glasses between them, which was a college record.

Not every Society dinner involves such a Lucullan orgy but they all provide splendid gastronomic training. The members of the dinner committee command facilities such as few private houses now enjoy. They have a comparatively large amount of money to play with. They learn not only to balance a menu, but also to administer a dinner party – how to arrange the flowers, how many servants to employ, how to solve the knotty problems of the seating plan, how to cope with a crisis when the port runs out, or the pudding surprise starts to melt, or the wines are lagging behind their proper courses. They learn to avoid all those little things which spoil the enjoyment of a dinner as it should be. Unlike other hosts, they also have the benefit of immediate and uninhibited criticism from their guests.

Gracious living may be undemocratic and reactionary, but it is a kind of education; an education with its roots deep in the vine-bearing soil of western Europe. As one undergraduate put it: 'If Oxford has taught me nothing else, it has taught me to prefer a silver salt-cellar which doesn't pour to a plastic one which does.' There might be two opinions about the value of that lesson, but it is very close to the heart of Oxford. Our greatest scholars have always been comfortable men, with messy old pipes and messy old gowns, fond of books and bottles and good fellowship, ready enough to ask with Peacock's gentle irony:

How can a man, in his life of a span,
Do anything better than dine?

Spring 1956

145

Entrées

Old Compton's Fancy, November

The noble pheasant has exerted his curious *liebestod* spell upon the hunter ever since the Romans first encountered him in the valley of the Pharsalus. He is linked to us by that doomed and destructive love which Hemingway has so often attempted to convey in his descriptions of the chase.

Fox-hunting, Old Compton holds, is marred by a lamentable lack of nobility in the fox; but the pheasant, like the salmon, is a prince; and when he's dead, regret tinges your exultation. His plumage lights our winters; his courage and devotion to his family are an example to us all; his voice is magical. The only problem is how to cook him worthily.

The English conventional method of cooking pheasant does, in Old Compton's opinion, monstrous injustice to the bird. For his part, he ties plenty of fat bacon over its breast and first browns it well in plenty of butter. Meanwhile, in another pan he fries chopped-up bacon, in due course adding shredded uncooked cabbage which he flavours with pepper, salt and a good pinch of thyme. He turns the cabbage carefully till it is all of a brilliant green. Then he adds perhaps a cup of good stock, covers the pan and lowers the flame.

After a few moments, he takes the pheasant (which in a moment of exuberance he may have flambé), lays it gently to doze upon the bed

149

of cabbage, adding the precious liquid in which it has cooked so far. During the last twenty minutes of cooking, he adds some fine peeled and cooked Spanish or Italian chestnuts – these should still be firm when added – and sections of a large smoked sausage of the Strasburg sort. No great bird ever enjoyed a more worthy pyre.

Winter 1960

Meals to Remember

Ann Bridge

Ann Bridge (Lady O'Malley) had a strenuous old-fashioned schoolroom education which included French, German, Italian, Latin and Greek. When she married a diplomatist the modern languages served her well, as did Latin and Greek in her two great interests, archaeology and botany. Of her twenty books, seventeen are novels; four were Book Society 'Choices', and three, Choices of the Literary Guild of America.

The food and drink are an important element of meals remembered, and so, very often, is the company; but the *mis en scène* can also add to one's pleasure, especially if one has a taste for contrasts.

* * *

In September I was in Burgos, and Bertram Jerram, then assistant to Sir Robert Hodgson, our 'agent' to General Franco during the Spanish Civil War, invited quite a party of people to luncheon in a Spanish country inn far out in the sierras, where he said the food was original, and rather good. He telegraphed four days in advance, telling the inn-keeper to prepare for twelve guests – but Spain being Spain, when our cars had ploughed through deep clayey mud along narrow tracks to the noble stone-built village and drew up in a cold rain before the inn, we found ourselves quite unexpected; the telegram had never arrived!

Of course we were warmly welcomed – Spain again being Spain; and extraordinary scenes then ensued. We were ushered into a large, rather bare room, with hard chairs and a long walnut table, on which were at once set glasses and many bottles of home-brewed anisette while bare-legged, wild-haired girls hurried in with brushwood and small logs, and hastily kindled a blazing fire in the huge chimney-place. We were glad of this, for the room was cold and we were chilled after the long slow drive; but I was enchanted by the bottles of the liqueur. Into each had been stuffed a branch of *Carum carvi*, the wild caraway, complete with its umbelliferous flower-head; the whole had become whitely encrusted with sugar, a snowy plant in a bottle. It was a rather syrupy drink, but strong and good. While the fire was burning up I took my glass to the window. In the yard outside the innkeeper was selecting chickens for our lunch; boys chased and snatched cockerels and brought them to him; he felt each one carefully, flung some aside, and expertly wrung the necks of others, which were carried into the kitchen.

These hasty preparations did not worry me. If a chicken is cooked before it has time to get cold, it is never tough; only gelatinous, and lacking the flavour of a well-hung bird. But I could see that these chickens had game blood in them, so they would be tasty anyhow. However, by the time they were plucked, drawn, and cooked, there would obviously be at least an hour's delay before we ate, so presently, inveterately curious, I made my way to the kitchen. This was something straight out of Don Quixote. In a huge low-ceilinged room a vast scrubbed table ran down the centre, with an immense open fire above which hung a cauldron of soup, and spits in front. Endless women with harsh splendid Spanish faces were plucking birds, chopping herbs, and preparing vegetables; a small boy turned the spit on which our chickens were roasting, constantly added to as more were made ready. A noble scene, and not a common one.

The lunch, when it came, was good – a splendid bean soup made with strong stock, the chickens, and a hot compôte of apricots laced with the local brandy; also plenty of red country wine, which had a curious flinty flavour. It was all served by the bare-legged women and girls – very unlike the demure perfection of Charles Mendl's Paris flat.

Winter 1960

Meals to Remember

wild goose breasts in toffee ... Madeira 1851 ... woodcock
on crumpets ...

James Robertson-Justice

After Marlborough and Bonn University, had, to quote his own words,
'a career undistinguished but varied, some three score jobs in different
parts of the world.' For all that, made an indelible mark in films as the
burly and irascible senior surgeon, Sir Lancelot Spratt, scourge of
incompetent juniors, who whirlwinded his way through St Swithins.

Kept his own falcons; invented a rocket-propelled net for bird
marking; and wrote not undistinguished papers on ornithology,
ecology, and conservation.

Of the meals I have eaten since the war, the one I shall always
remember (for have I not the menu propped up in front of me as I
write, though should I ever be so graceless as to forget it, let my right
hand forget her cunning) was a luncheon given two years ago by
Roger Slade, the retiring Master of the Ironmongers Company, to

some twenty-five of his friends. We took luncheon at an enormous circular table, covered, be it noted, by a splendid linen tablecloth, and in the ante-room of the Ironmongers' Hall, where the plate of that ancient Company was displayed for the pleasure of our eyes.

The melon frappé was accompanied by a Madeira of 1851 for which there exist no superlatives to do anything like justice to its description. Alas! there is no more of it. A mousse of salmon and salad was escorted by a Brauneberger Burgeslay Riesling of 1949, a splendid Moselle and a most exquisitely prepared fish. The memory of the next course induces such a feeling of hunger that I can hardly bear to write about it, seeing that I am about to dine, but we had tiny lamb cutlets, grilled, with French beans and new potatoes, and a Lafite (*nomen praeclarissimum*) of 1929 about which I defy any wine drinker to be less than lyrical. A gooseberry 'Yce' was married to an Yquem of 1923, a marriage straight from the Almanach de Gotha, and, after a savoury of Devils on Horseback, we had English hot-house peaches and a Taylor 1924 port. The brandy with which this feast ended was a thirty-year-old Hine, and of the same standard as the rest of it. The shocked face of the Beadle when the assembled company burst, at a prearranged signal, into the chorus of 'Any Old Iron' but changing to a delighted smile of appreciation, was not the least of the pleasures of this splendid luncheon.

* * *

My wife has been known to produce a meal which has delighted the *cognoscenti*, and, if I may be permitted a blast on the trumpet, I have produced one or two myself. There was an occasion, one January, in a motor-boat and the middle of the Wash, when, during intervals between sallies in a duck punt, and for the delectation of five of us, she produced crisp (the operative word) bacon, and immaculately fried eggs – not the greasy, pinguid objects masquerading under that name as served in so many British hotels, but fried eggs to perfection, and all on a primus stove, and, thereafter, a cold roast pheasant which had been shot exactly six weeks before, and was, without exception, the finest cold roast pheasant I have ever eaten. It may be remarked, in parenthesis, that it was a melanistic mutant cock, a bird of the year, and that some of its feathers still decorate my falcon's hoods. This, washed down with a bottle of Swedish acquavit, swopped for a score of wigeon with the skipper of a German timber vessel bound for Boston, but waiting for the tide, made a meal worthy of remembrance.

I have no space to describe the odd meal where great discoveries were made, such as the occasion when I cooked wild goose breasts in toffee for Peter Scott and Gavin (Harpoon at a Venture) Maxwell, but, however irreverent, and misleading the name of the dish, it has now become, from a more or less accidental beginning, a staple of my own table.

But I would like to finish with the menu of a luncheon I gave myself not so long ago. Turtle soup, Madeira, Old Bual. Cold Salmon (a very late, but fresh run fish, caught, I regret not at all to say, out of season and, to my mind, the acid test of a cook's skill) salad, Brauneberger Juffer Spaetlese, 1949, and two woodcock (each!) not, as usual, on toast, but on crumpets – a discovery which I am proud to have made in the interests of gastronomy – with a Richebourg 1947, and, again, *nomen praeclarissimum*, a blue Cheshire followed by Graham's Six Grapes, the best Tawny port I have yet encountered.

Winter 1955

Mustard

(1973 was the 150th foundation anniversary of J. & J. Colman of Norwich, mustardeers extraordinary)

Geoffrey Godbert

In plant, seed or condiment form, mustard boasts a commendable pedigree, backed up by documentary evidence. In 584 BC Pythagoras gave it a write-up, as did the physician, Hippocrates, about 100 years later. Still in the BCs, the Emperor Darius is reputed to have sent Alexander the Great a bag of sesame seed, symbolising the numbers mustered within his army. Alexander responded with a sack of mustard seed to indicate not only the number, but the fiery energy of his soldiers. They won – conclusively.

On one text alone from the New Testament, sermons have resounded from pulpits of all denominations for near 2,000 years.

Mustard continued to loom large in medieval reflection; and with good reason – most basic foods, particularly meat, were pretty putrid by the time they were brought to table. Camouflage seasoning was the answer. When, in 1336, the Duke of Burgundy entertained King Philip VI of France to a banquet, seventy gallons of mustard were consumed. Pope John XXII was moved to create one of his favourites 'First Mustardeer'. The man must have put on such airs that the saying long survived of any swollenheaded person, '*Il se croit le premier moutardier du Pape*'.

In France there was a popular rhyme which, translated, went:
From three things good Lord protect us:
   Salt Silverside without fresh mustard:
   A serving man who can't be trusted:
   A woman's face with paint encrusted.

In England, Tewkesbury was famed for its mustard which was ground into a paste, presumably with locally grown wine, or vinegar from it, then put in earthenware pots and covered with pieces of parchment collected from old, unwanted letters or deeds. It was in 1380 that Wycliffe, delivering himself of a final rebuke during a theological dispute, came out with, 'These letters may do good to cover mustard pots, but not to bring men to bliss'.

Shakespeare had one of his characters, in Henry IV, part I, referred to as having 'wit as thick as Tewkesbury mustard'. There is, incidentally, an ingenious argument put forward, by those with time on their hands, that whereas Shakespeare mentions mustard several times in his works and Bacon none in his, then Bacon cannot have written Shakespeare's plays.

One assumes that mustard pastes were brown, or *brassica nigra* mustard, for the medical botanist Gerarde says in the days of Queen Elizabeth that Garden White mustard had not become common, and that he had distributed it to different parts of England to make it more known.

However, some mustard must have been used in powder form, for there are references to mustard querns in 1356, which means that mustard was ground over the food at table, as we use a pepper mill today.

It is not clear when powder mustard became a commercial article, but until 1720 it must have been prepared by pounding in a mortar and carrying out a rough separation from the skin. In this year it is believed that a Mrs Clements, of Durham, who had conceived the idea of grinding the seed and sifting it in the same manner as flour from wheat, began the first national sales campaign. She kept her secret for many years, and supplied the principal parts of the Kingdom, especially London. King George I became an appreciative patron.

The East coast of England, the drier side of the country, became the mustard growing area, and mustard mills grew up from Durham down to Essex.

The year 1823 was quite momentous: war began between France and Spain; work began on building the British Museum; the US President Monroe introduced his Doctrine (closing the American continents to colonial settlements by non-American Powers); and Jeremiah Colman, who had taken over a Norwich mustard factory, took into partnership his nephew James Colman and thus established the firm of J. & J. Colman – a name to become universally identified with mustard. An early adherent to the potential of advertising, Colman's attained a major impact in 1926 with a novelty campaign. This, known as 'The Mustard Club', attained overnight mass popularity and is still contemplated with nostalgia by older members of the advertising world – and, more importantly, of the public.

Autumn 1972

Camaraderie of the Vendange

Stuart Ross brings to life the hardships and happiness of the *Vendange*.

Madame said, as I suggested a separate plate might be appropriate for my vegetables, 'You really are more bloody French than the French.'

I concede there is often an element of truth in some of her more abrasive generalisations. I accept a preference for vegetables as a separate course. The flavour of leaf spinach for example should not be confused with an entrecôte. Cheese before the sweet warrants another glass of claret and makes sense. True, I am addicted to Bordeaux wines and find myself frighteningly vulnerable to the vivacity of French women. True, French music charms me and I am as much haunted by the voices of Piaf and Jacques Brel as I am by the music of Debussy or Saint-Saens.

Francophile I may be but I am in no way blind to their faults. There is absolutely no excuse for their irritating habit of crumbling bread all over the table and floor when a civilised side-plate is an obvious

157

solution. Their summer obsession with the Tour de France palls on one. Wobbling bicycles and the *maillot jaune* – a yellow T-shirt the victor wears – cannot compare with the elegance of white flannelled figures playing at Lords. Their passion for pétanque or boule cannot rival the glories of a cover-drive or the audacity of a sweep to leg.

The summer of 1980 was diabolical. Not within living memory had the winds and rain torn at the vines with such unabated fury. Last summer was not a lot better. In the second week of July an occasional log fire was welcome – normally we are outside until dusk. A glass of *pineau* (a brandy-based drink exclusively from the two Charente Departments of France) restored circulation and morale whereas iced sangria in the shade of the lime tree is the norm before lunch at this time of the year.

But to get to the real feel of the grape one must get to the roots of the subject. Discard the glossies with their euphuistic and often meaningless phraseology. Go into the vineyards and 'do' a vendange. I have watched it yearly. Our children, godchildren, nephews and their friends have all done it – some more than once. The going rate in 1981 was around 118 francs per day plus lunch. There is something rather special about the 'vendange'. It produces a team spirit and a willingness to work conscientiously without supervision among people of different ages, sexes and backgrounds. It produces a humour and camaraderie all its own. Politicians might benefit were they to study the motivating reasons. Their 'summits' in exotic places seem to lose touch with the basics. It is doubtful also whether many of our British shop stewards have been 'vendangeurs' – more's the pity.

The first day's work is without doubt the worst. 'Completely knackered' was how our eighteen-year-old nephew described his general well-being at the end of his first ten hour stint (two hours off for lunch). A hot bath, a visit to the local *estaminet* to meet his fellow workers and he returned slightly less 'knackered' but infinitely more ebullient.

The rows of vines are usually picked by two members of the *équipe*. One on one side and one on the other. In fact the bunches of grapes are not picked but are cut with secateurs. Nowadays they are thrown into plastic buckets, transferred to a tractor-pulled wagon which can pass up and down the *rangs* and this dictates the distance between the rows of vines. The grapes are then transported to the *pressoir* usually located in an outbuilding of the farm. The extracted juice runs into *cuves* where it is syphoned to others.

In 1979 I remember every spare barrel, vat and container was

brought into use to cope with an abundant supply. 1980 and 1981 have been relatively poor. A late summer and early frosts following Toussaint combined to make the task of 'vendangeing' tough and exacting work. They stuck to it in all weathers with biting cold winds from the north one minute giving way to hot sunshine the next.

The average wine produced by a single vine is one litre. A white grape produces three times this amount. A rough rule of thumb is that one hectare (2.47 acres) is planted with 4500 vines.

Day followed day in the vineyards. Gossip was exchanged. Friendships among the young deepened. A romance was born. In three weeks the job was done. Pay-day arrived.

The *jour du loi* is unlike any other pay-day. The farmer and his wife lay on a celebration lunch and vie with their neighbours to produce a meal the 'vendangeurs' will enjoy and remember. It starts around midday and goes on for four or five hours – even longer. To survive the succession of courses and cornucopia of wine is no mean achievement. Anyone who takes their own bottles is presented with a dozen bottles or so of 'their' vintage.

High labour costs as you can see are beginning to price the individual picker out of the market – as in so many other industries.

Sadly the machine, although still to be perfected, is slowly but surely replacing manual labour.

Today a wealth of humour and pride goes into wine-making. There is personality, character and individualism enshrined in every bottle. For me, when the day of automation finally arrives, the colour and light reflected from a glass of wine will be sterile – lacking human warmth and laughter. As the liquid is reverently poured from bottle to crystal glass (Baccarat or St Louis for preference) that mischievous little wink of welcome will be missing.

Could I even yet become a writer on wine?

Summer, 1982

Turkey in its Pride

'Probably the earliest European drawing of a turkey in existence'

Sir George Bellew

The birds which, at Christmas, play unwittingly so important a part, were first brought to Europe at the beginning of the sixteenth century. Some say this great event was the work of one Pedro Nino who found them in Cumano in north Venezuela in 1499 and brought them back to Spain in the year following; others say that the honour goes to that renowned mariner, Sebastian Cabot, who brought them back from Mexico, the land of the Montezumas, in about 1520.

Why they are called turkeys is a little uncertain. Possibly their original Aztec name sounded something like that. The country called Turkey has apparently nothing to do with it.

Prior to the days of Cabot, that is, in the fourteenth and fifteenth centuries, peacock was the chef d'oeuvre on festive occasions on the tables of the great. Mr Everyman had goose. During the next two centuries the aristocratic peacock steadily lost favour and turkey took its place. It was not, however, until the eighteenth century that Mr Everyman had turkey too.

The Crest (for that is what it is) which accompanies these few words, is taken from a record in the College of Arms, dated 1550, in which year 'a turkey in its pride' was granted as a Crest to William Stickland of Boynton on the Wold. The original drawing is, as you can see, crude, obviously the work of a great French artist, exciting, the work of a child, or even appetising, according to the way you look at it; but in any case it has the distinction of not improbably being the earliest European pictorial representation of a turkey in existence. It was given to William Strickland as a Crest because so it is said, he accompanied Cabot to Central America and probably, therefore, brought the first turkeys to England.

Winter 1955

The Honest Sonsie Haggis

D. England

To the skirl of bagpipes and the swirl of the kilts, on every Burns Night, 25 January, all over the English-speaking world, the most important item of the feast is brought in – the haggis. And over it are recited the ever-memorable lines 'To a Haggis':

> O what a glorious sight,
> Warm-reekin', rich!

– and also that incomparable tribute:

> Fair fa' your honest sonsie face,
> Great chieftain o' the puddin'-race!
> Aboon them a' ye tak your place,
> Painch, tripe, or thairm:
> Weel are ye wordy o' a grace
> As lang's my arm.

In recent years the Scots have succeeded in their ambition – putting haggis, that dish which has inspired immense reverence and just as much ribaldry, on the export list. 'The best thing to do with it', an Englishman rudely remarked. On occasion Americans have been unsympathetic towards it, and some Canadians have treated it with less than reverence.

This was when criminals so far stooped in depredation and degradation as to use the honest, sonsie haggis to deaden the sound of an exploding safe. And that safe in the store of J. Inglis Reid, Vancouver, maker of haggis! This criminal insult to the haggis was laid bare in court, and the prosecutor properly declared the felony proved: 'there must be no reverence left in the criminal mind'.

Once a haggis weighing 83 lb, a really comely size, was despatched from Prestwick to New York. After display in the British Travel Association window, Madison Avenue, it was divided between the Burns Societies in the United States.

When a Scots merchant conveyed a couple of haggis to Seattle in an earlier attempt to popularise the historic concoction, a Customs official bluntly commented: 'We won't taste it. Food experts will make a chemical test'. This was duly carried out, and Customs declared a twenty-five per cent duty would be imposed on the haggis, officially classified as 'pudding or hash made of vegetables and meat'. That was something, anyway, for the haggis was acknowledged as eatable.

Another indignity once befell the haggis at a dinner of St Andrew's Club, London, before 500 Scots. It was being carried round on a trencher in traditional fashion by two chefs to the strains of 'Brose and Butter', played by a Pipe Major of the King's Own Scottish Borderers, when the awful thing happened.

The chefs, apparently overcome by the enthusiastic reception of the assembled host, accidentally tipped the platter and the great chieftain o' the puddin' race dropped to the floor. In such a trial it proved its mettle, for it bounced but did not break!

Why should one record such minor tragedies? The reason is that the haggis is regarded as Scotland's most historic dish, though nowadays a mystery to everyone born south of the Border. So ancient is it that it is difficult to say when and where it did originate. Mary Queen of Scots is said to have known all about it, but strangely enough, and hard for Scots to believe, at the time of Cromwell this dish, which today is understood to be barely compatible with an Englishman remaining at table, was very common in England. The writer of a work called the 'English Housewife', just 300 years back, said oatmeal could be mixed with the liver of sheep, calf, or pig, thus making 'that pudding which is called haggas, or haggus, of whose goodness it is in vain to boast because there is hardly to be found a man that does not affect them'.

There must surely be something out of the ordinary in a dish which has existed so long and outlived its critics. The late Professor Saintsbury thought so. In his opinion, 'People who regard haggis and sheep's head as things that the lips should not allow to enter them and the tongue should refuse to mention are, begging their pardon, fools.'

As for the actual recipe, many a method has been claimed as the one and only. In brief, the haggis is concocted of the heart, liver, lungs and sometimes the intestines of a sheep, mixed with oatmeal, onions, suet and seasoning. The whole mixture is boiled in the coat of a sheep's stomach, which has been previously soaked in salt water, boiled, and scraped. One fine old Scottish gentleman declared: 'Serve with old whisky; or (if greatly daring) with Atholl brose, a mixture of equal parts of whisky, cream, and honey.'

Well, there's the haggis, which one Scotsman described as 'Fine, confused eating'. An Englishman more unkindly declared it was a dish containing everything of the sheep – except the mutton.

Winter 1962

Brigadier R.F. Johnson

Haggess: this old *Norfolk* dish is described in a family recipe book dating from the seventeenth century.

A calf's heart (or sheep's) with the liver and lights. Seethe together $\frac{1}{2}$ hour. Set aside a portion of ye liver (about a $\frac{1}{4}$) till it is cooled. Hash the rest fine. Place in a wide bason, mixing in the crumb of a French roll soak'd in cream, 1 lb. beef suet chopp'd fine, $\frac{1}{2}$ a nutmeg grated, beaten cinnamon, cloves, some chopp'd onion or shalot as lik'd. 1 lb. raisins, stoned and chopp'd, yolks of three eggs, some chitterlings well clean'd and cut into slips, several peppers and salt to taste and enough oatmeal to give ye whole a proper consistence. Over all grate ye liver yt was first set aside. Into the mixture stir $\frac{1}{2}$ pint (or a little more) bouillon or stock. Some say sweet wine is better.

Then take the stomach or paunch, yt has been wash'd entirely clean with spring water both inside and out, dry'd and left inside-out till requir'd. Put in ye mixture till enough therein to leave room for ye mixture to swell when boiling.

Sew up ye paunch with packthread and prick it all over with a coarse needle.

Boil 3 hours.

Winter 1962

Bad Wines I Have Loved

Bruce Blunt

There are as many degrees of badness in wines as there are degrees of goodness. When you think of the enormous range of experience which lies between a Richebourg, for instance, and a Château Pontet-Canet, this is rather a forbidding thought.

But bad wines can be fun.

I am not referring now to wines which are bad because they have been made by bad men. These are dull and slimy wines which are intended to deceive. They commit petty theft and hope to get away with it.

The interesting bad wines are the bolder ones, the larger criminals which commit excesses from exuberance or rebellion. They are the really naughty wines and, as in the human race, can be so much more entertaining than the nice ones.

We all know those dapper, precise wines which you would never call on for a song. They are so well-tailored that you cannot fault them; but you cannot love them very much.

I once came across a black wine of Aragon which was the bad man of the district. It had committed several murders. It very nearly murdered me.

It was a wine of such astounding arrogance that you would never think it was on sale for a few pence a glass in the local bars. It was so dark and brawny that it took you by the throat. It did not care what it tasted like. Its ferocity was a challenge.

In a burst of bravado I took up the challenge. This ruffian wine was not a pleasure to drink. It was a pleasure to fight. It carried the kick of a mule. To this day I am not certain whether it was a mule or the wine which landed me in the ditch where I was found.

The most remarkable character which I have ever met in wines was a Pommard les Rugiens of 1942. But then, it was made by the most remarkable character among wine-makers whom I have ever known.

This is Monsieur Félix Clerget, proprietor at Pommard, Corton, Clos de Vougeot and goodness knows where else beside. Barrister, sculptor, painter, the owner of a well-stored cellar and a well-stored mind, a brilliant talker, gay companion and the most generous of hosts, Félix could have made his mark in almost any calling that he might have chosen. He chose wine.

A taste for Gallo-Roman antiquity accounts for several odd fragments of stone which lie about the courtyard of his house at Pommard. A similar taste for antiquity accounts for the wine of which I write. Fired with an ambition to make a wine in the fearless old fashion of his ancestors, he decided to experiment with this Pommard. Without any fining or racking, or addition or subtraction of any kind, this wine was made, stored and finally bottled in its absolutely primitive state.

The result was interesting and even surprising.

The wine had the unusual quality that no two bottles ever tasted alike.

It was known as the Vin du Diable and was kept all by itself in a small inner cellar which became the Cave du Diable. This precaution was probably taken so that its wayward conduct might not affect the behaviour of the more conventional wines in the other cellars.

I first tasted this unpredictable wine in 1945, when it was still quite young in bottle.

The first bottle which Félix opened was deceptively sedate. From one's glass arose that full and fruity perfume of Pommard, and the taste of the wine gave promise of a pleasant Rugiens in its maturity.

When the next bottle was opened, there was an aroma like that which sometimes assails the nostrils on a country road when a silage pit has just been opened on a good scenting day.

The third bottle gave the impression that it would shortly have burst if the agonised wine had not been released by the drawing of the cork.

On further tasting over the years, I quite fell in love with this child of nature.

One of the harshest wines which I can remember was a red Meursault of 1937. When it was young it bit you as you drank. It rasped the throat. It was a file of a wine.

This is one of the very few red wines of Meursault and its behaviour made me glad that most of the Meursault vineyards are planted with white grapes.

Then there was a very different wine which used to fascinate me. It was a white wine of Monthelie, but it was made with a mixture of some outlawed grapes which gave it such a peculiar flavour that it brought the days of my childhood back to me. It tasted just like dear old grannie's parsnip wine.

Whenever I went to its cellar I would taste it to see if it could possibly get any worse. It never did. And it never got any better.

Summer 1955

Old Compton's Fancy, April

Mme Bataille's Alarming Health Notes

With the winter apparently interminable we were pleased to see that our globe artichokes are still surviving.

I once saw an advertisement by the Brittany Information Bureau of London glorifying the artichoke – 'Tonight, excite his imagination as well as his palate.' Obviously, I thought, they're selling it as an aphrodisiac.

We had also learnt from a regular feature for hypochondriacs in that otherwise monstrous weekly scandal sheet, *France Dimanche*, that the artichoke 'calms the rheumatisms'. What's more, it dissolves excess cholestrol in the blood and so counteracts the effect of melted butter, if you prefer that to any of the sauces the British artichoke promoter considers you should serve. (Perhaps that's where the aphrodisiac lies – in vinaigrette for instance.)

Mme Bataille, who writes these helpful but sometimes alarming health notes, continues with assurances that the cucumber reduces the anxiety, the spinach fortifies the heart (but is useless for the fragile livers and the kidneys), the celery prevents the 'flu, the mushroom

166

gives the muscle, the carrot improves the view, the cabbage combats the ulcer in the *estomac*; but no petit pois if you suffer the colitis, or haricots verts if you have some rheumatisms, or garlic if you lack the tension. On the other hand for the diabetics the onion is recommended (it contains, it is said, the same properties as insulin as a means of lowering the sugar in the blood). The turnip, Mme Bataille continues, drives away the acne, the pumpkin calms the piles, and asparagus the eczema. And finally the aubergine is unbeatable for the slimming.

Summer 1979

Eating Your Way Through the Bottom of the World

Peter Johnson on the gastronomic pleasures and perils of being a travel writer in the Antipodes.

Jet-lagged, overweight and with a bruise on my navel from buckling and unbuckling seat-belts after thirty-eight landings and take-offs in eighteen days, I returned from a maiden antipodean visit with a dire warning to anyone planning to follow in my footsteps: If you want to bust your calorie curbs, go to New Zealand.

I now know what the Kiwis did with the mountain of lamb, beef, butter, and cheese left on their hands when Britain turned its back and joined the Common Market. They set about eating it. Officially they will tell you that they have found fresh markets in the Far East, South-East Asia and the Middle East. But take it from me, that's all malarkey: what they are doing is putting it on the plates in Pacific-sized portions as part of a sinister plot based on the theory that an army of tourists marches on its stomach.

Prompted by this discovery, I offer a quick guide to eating your way through the bottom of the world, flagging the high-spots and the pitfalls alike.

A high-spot (undoubtedly, at 35,000 feet, it had to be) was the restaurant run by Lana, Bluey, Janice and John. Low-spots included the Regent Tea Rooms in Otorohanga and the bus station cafeteria in Hamilton. But first, the good news.

The L.B.J. & J. restaurant was in a spanking new Jumbo jet speeding its way over the Pacific, the delivery flight from Boeing in Seattle of Air New Zealand's first 747; the talented quartet were part of the cabin crew. I had found promise of the culinary delights of the 'Flying Kiwi' in a small volume, *The Breakfast Book*, by David St. John Thomas, strategically thrust into my hands by an airline PR man before take-off. 'Some airlines really do try harder,' writes Thomas, and among these he numbers Air New Zealand, to whom he awards ninety-one marks out of 100 on 'an enviable record for service and – yes – culinary art.'

With £6 million worth of Rolls-Royce engines propelling me towards New Zealand at 400 miles an hour, I sampled some of this art at breakfast time on Thursday, or was it Friday? I really don't know because the international dateline robbed me of a day somewhere in the first course, iced orange juice served with a slice of fresh orange and a maraschino cherry. It was followed by a Polynesian fruit salad, with fresh cream if I had wanted it.

Then a choice of mahi mahi grenobloise, mushroom omelette or poached egg americaine; coward, I settled for the omelette, cooked there and then by John, but Janice insisted that I also try the mahi mahi, a deliciously spiced Hawaiian fish. There were hot rolls, croissants or toast, and – as author Thomas found – 'what New Zealanders (and Australians) call a Devonshire Tea for breakfast: fresh scones, strawberry jam and cream, whipped and not scalded as in an English Devonshire cream tea.' Janice, Janice, what about my weight problem?

Was it, I enquired, special fare for a special flight that carried VIPs and a posse of free-loading journalists like myself? It was, they assured me, 'a normal first-class breakfast'. Well, full marks – even though the four-star image was slightly dented when, before landing, a tray of boiled sweets was offered with the beguiling Kiwi invitation, 'D'y'wanna lollie?'

Don't go to New Zealand without feasting yourself at a Maori 'hangi' in which the meat and vegetables are cooked by a steam process in a pit of hot stones laid in the ground. The tradition produces some very big Maoris, viz. the All Blacks.

Lamb, of course, is a must. It has to be with three million people and sixty-six million sheep. As a token of respect to the national larder – I noticed – the Speaker's chair in parliament is completely lined, back, arms and seat, with sheepskin.

A veil will be drawn over the Hamilton bus station cafeteria. At least, the Regent Tea Rooms in Otorohanga, ninety-five miles from

Auckland, have a rugged charm, being set in a colonaded High Street reminiscent of the Wild West. There is no reason why a culinary guide should include the Regent Tea Rooms except that they were on obligatory lunchtime 'refreshment and comfort' stop on a bus excursion from Auckland to Rotorua, one of the few land journeys of my tour. I ordered fish and chips and have nothing more to say about the matter.

My companion settled for 'ham salad' – and got ham, a lettuce leaf, a mountain of boiled potatoes and a swamp of mushy peas. A New Zealand journalist returning after five years' absence, she had forgotten that a 'salad' means any dish with cold meat. In its defence, Otorohanga (pop. 2,000) is cheap and exceedingly cheerful – and helpings are characteristically generous.

Where food is downbeat in New Zealand much of the blame can arguably be placed on the British heritage. Sandwiches are, in an oddly comforting way, British to the core: sad, uninspired and infuriatingly clingfoil-wrapped. There is a plethora of 'cafeterias' where battery snackers take their nourishment by lifting flaps on tiers of plastic hutches.

Deep was my chagrin when, arriving at the splendid Hermitage Hotel – set in the breathtaking scenery of Mount Cook area, I was offered at the witching hour of 2 p.m. the only hot food still on the menu: the cafeteria's plastic-clad steak pies. This is silly as the hotel is capable of good, French-based cuisine, as dinner in the restaurant proved that evening.

The scene changes and the flying gourmet moves 125 miles east across South Island to ever-so-English Christchurch – and some fine fare for the most discerning trencherman in a most unlikely setting, an ex-servicemen's club. The Returned Services Club at Christchurch looks like any thriving social club in the north-east of England.

'And so it should; we're knee deep in Poms,' said my host. English names, English faces, and beer going down by the jug as the Queen smiles benignly from above the bar. But the restaurant is something to write home to Blighty about, despite the self-service and the canteen decor.

Its star dish comes from Bluff. Bluff is the southernmost point of mainland New Zealand. It has Ocean Beach, Lookout Point, a chilly climate, more than its share of cold-kneed Scots in kilts – and oysters. Bluff is renowned for its oysters. At the Christchurch RSC you can dine on a dozen Bluffs and a huge, succulent Aberdeen Angus steak and still get change from a fiver.

One dark and stormy night the boys and girls were whooping it up in the Diggins Saloon at Queenstown, a mountain fastness in the gold-mining country. Don, the government tourist manager, was there; so too were Dale the back-country safari man, Heather and Trevor who run the jet boats on the Shotover River, and a jolly Friday night bunch of game and fishing rangers, mountain guides and lake-steamer men. Kiwi beer at 70p a jug was going down faster than the Sutherland Falls up on the Great Divide.

'What's your number?' I was asked.

I looked at my raffle ticket – 'Sixty-five.'

'You've won the raffle, sport,' said Joe O'Connell, who is caretaker at the local primary school and fund-raiser for the Otago Wanderers cricket team. He handed me a bucket of three dozen Bluff oysters sloshing about in water. We finished them in two minutes flat, dipping our hands in the water and scooping them out'.

Then we toasted the success of the Wanderers on their forthcoming tour to London and the Home Counties – the reason for the fund-raising raffle. So if you happened to see a team of rangy, sunburned mountain men clouting sixes over the village green this summer, you'll know it was my oysters that helped send them there.

Summer 1982

Meals to Remember

some tales of the long fork

D.B. Wyndham Lewis

Self-assessment

Author, journalist and (at full moon) critic. Fellow, for some reason, of the Royal Society of Literature. Columnist for some years in the London *Daily Express*, *Daily Mail*, *News Chronicle*, and *Tatler*. Has even made the *New Yorker*, and, before they tightened things up, had a photograph in *Time*. Also writes books, but who doesn't? Favourably spoken of in the trade for integrity, though not often.

Interested in cheese, cats, women, French novels and the exquisite keyboard music of Couperin the Great. Also in Liberals, BBC comics, critics drunk and sober, tiny actresses with big appealing eyes, and in general all wild, wayward, furry things wounded by Life.

Believes that when all's said and done there are few nobler things on earth than the love of a dear old silver-haired publisher, knowing all, enduring all, forgiving all.

A meal to be remembered, in its modest way, and particularly for its surprise-value, was a hasty one taken not long ago on the Great North Road between London and York. We stopped for half an hour at that once-famous coaching inn the Bell at Stilton. More than one picaresque eighteenth-century novelist has a scene at the Bell, usually ending in great tumult and bobbery round about 2 a.m.; gentlemen and noblemen diving hastily in and out of strange beds and whipping out rapiers on the staircase, amid a tempest of screams and oaths and a hail of candlesticks, goblets, bootjacks, pewter-pots, and intimate chinaware. This liveliness is vanished, alas. The inn itself is not what it was. Betty and Sukey and Moll and the other saucy apple-cheeked chambermaids who used to romp with Britain's gentry have tripped long since into limbo, and those two rival benefactresses of the human race who claim the invention of Stilton Cheese – Mrs Orton and Mrs Paulet, bless their bonny red faces – have been dust for three centuries. However, the surprise came swiftly. For at least a lifetime or two it was well known that the last place in England to find Stilton cheese was at the Bell in Stilton; G.K. Chesterton even wrote a lament about it, beginning, 'Stilton! Thou shouldst be living at this hour.' But lo and look ye! Having playfully asked for it and expecting a homely

brush-off, we got the cheese instead – the real thing, produced instantly, ripe and enticing, with crusty new bread, fresh butter, and a foaming tankard. There is no better kind of nutrition-intake, perhaps, on earth. Well, practically. Well, in a way.

And again, one winter night in the Rue Montorgeuil near the Halles in Paris. The first-floor room of a dusky little restaurant, with rain lashing the panes; the patron, a bulky shirt-sleeved Norman, bearing in a great earthenware vessel of tripes à la mode de Caen composed with care by himself; a dinner lasting some four hours, and a company of four which included Belloc in top form; the wine, the talk, and the mirth. No doubt the place is vanished by now. I have never been near it since. The good times do not repeat themselves. Cecil Day Lewis has said it:

> Do not expect again a phoenix hour,
> The triple-towered sky, the dove complaining,
> Sudden the rain of gold and heart's first ease ...

I hesitate about the fricassee of kid, or goat, in the little old town of Ripoll in the Spanish Pyrenees. It seems now to have been a luscious offering, perfectly mated to lashings of the rough red wine of Aragon, the music of rushing water nearby and the far-off plucking of a guitar. But we were very young, and we had come many miles that day on foot under a formidable sun. The tortilla, contrariwise, was detestable, though rich in eggs. They had put some local herb into it, probably plucked by the hag Celestina in the cold of the moon. An elderly witch was in the kitchen, weaving spells, as we went out. She said, 'The tortilla is not to your Graces' liking?' and my Spanish-speaking companion said: 'Mother, it is not of this earth.' To which the old witch crone replied: 'Go with God, knights,' and we left her, bent double and cackling like the Fairy Carabosse. But her cookery was not deliberately lethal, whereas I recall a remote hell-kitchen in Sussex which specialised in what seemed to be roast vampire-bats served with poison-ivy.

Winter 1958

Meals to Remember

'in two out of three meals remembered, people and places, rather than the food and wine consumed, come more readily into focus …'

Baron

Second Lt Baron Stirling Henry Nahum (from Tripoli) was larger than life. Flair, optimism and persistence brought him to the top in photography. The war brought him a shattered left arm and an MBE. An inveterate both-ends-of-the-candle burner, he adored lavish parties, worked ceaselessly recording the famous, kept love-birds and a monkey in his salon, loved cricket and beautiful girls, raced horses and played a kind of golf all his own.

Hollywood

Lunch in a film studio restaurant is usually an unreal affair.

But when lunching in the Fox Studios in Hollywood with Marilyn Monroe, my attention was distracted neither by the company around us nor, for that matter, by the food in front of me.

Nor was the lily gilded; but wrapped in a towelled dressing-gown and face quite un-made up. Hugh French, her agent, who was with us, had previously warned me there was no chance of getting Marilyn to pose for me at that time. Half-way through a T-bone steak I made my plea and almost swallowed it whole when the answer came back: 'How would tomorrow do?' It did.

Bangkok

The feast was set superbly. Outside flowed the great river Chao Pya, busy with craft of every shape and size, while on the opposite bank was the huge tower of the temple of Wat Arun.

My host and hostess were Prince Chula Chakrabongse and his wife Lisba. Thirty or forty different dishes were arrayed on the table; all looked tempting. Yet it was with some reluctance that I broached them, for nearly all were carved in an exquisite fashion – cucumbers in the form of boats, apples in the form of birds ... the ingenuity displayed was fascinating and made one hesitate to demolish such things of beauty in so perfunctory a manner. An important Siamese meal takes five or six cooks three to four days to prepare.

London

Here, at last, is the one-in-every-four meal when the food and wine almost takes precedence in the memory. Needless to say, it was a stag dinner-party, in my Knightsbridge flat.

174

The conversation was commensurable with the company, which consisted of an actor, a journalist, two naval officers, a playwright, two editors, a restaurateur and two country-gentlemen.

The meal? My French maid, Jeanne, was at the top of her form. Caviar, then Scallops Provençale with garlic and parsley sauce as only the French know how; then poussins followed by oeufs à la neige. The wines Vodka, Montrachet 1943, Pomerol 1938, Château D'Yquem 1921. A Madeira 1862 and a sixty-year-old Cognac rounded the meal off.

Autumn 1955

The 'English' Breakfast

Lord Alastair Gordon

The English breakfast, even when taken at an early hour, is usually a substantial one.

The moral and physical welfare of mankind depends largely on its breakfast.... A being well fed and warmed is naturally on better terms with himself and his surroundings than those whose mind and body are being taxed by the discomfort and annoyance of badly cooked or insufficient food.

Mrs Beeton (1836-65)

It's the only meal that the British cannot ruin, so the saying goes. But now they have, by not having it at all. Tea, with toast and marmalade, or one of the faddy cereals, all eaten in a few minutes – what kind of a breakfast is that?

'Go to work on an egg' urges the Egg Marketing Board. What! *one* Egg?

This is not to be a social history of what or when people could afford to eat. It is to be a nostalgic wallow in that uniquely British institution of breakfast as a serious meal and as an entertainment. Other countries may now have taken it up with zest, but they are mere pasticheurs: *we* invented it and gave it status.

To be fair the first American breakfast I ate was the well-established waffles, maple syrup and bacon. Nursing the hangover I had had constructed for me the previous night, I thought I was going to be sick; judge of my relief and pleasure when I found this unlikely juxtaposition to be both delicious and nourishing. Not all good breakfasts are British.

Harrovian 'finds'

But to return to the real thing, before Mr Kellogg's wheat packets uniformly decorated the world's breakfast tables like a cluster of model skyscrapers. Traditionally at pre-war Harrow – several other schools followed much the same procedure – senior boys in each house had their own breakfast room – a kind of officers' mess – separate from the other ranks in the house dining room. This was known as finds or finding, for it was the job of the head fag, suitably funded, to buy the food from various shops which was then cooked in the house kitchens, usually by a team of junior fags. Just how lavish this food was depended on the wealth of the senior boys who each subscribed a messing fee. Rumour had it that in one house caviare was not infrequently served. Certainly it is true that all the trappings of the rich country house breakfast were in evidence on Sundays, when it was the custom to entertain senior chaps from other houses, and occasionally masters and their wives. These latter must have found it an ordeal to match the vast appetites and gusty conversation of muscular boys that early in the morning; especially in the summer, when the breakfast would end with strawberries and cream served fully an hour after the meal had started.

Porridge and herrings

The only sort of breakfast to match this kind of thing *habitually* is the Scottish one.

When I was young I spent an exhausting night on a West of Scotland herring drifter. At 5 a.m. I returned to the house where I was staying and dumped two dozen fresh caught fish on the kitchen table. Four hours later, after a short reviving sleep, I ate three of those herrings, grilled in oatmeal by an old Scots wifey. And the herrings were no more than part of it. The Scottish breakfast like so many of that Superior Nation's customs and traditions, is founded as much on historical fancy as historical fact. The Scots say porridge is better with salt than sugar. The true reason for the custom is that the Scots were so poor they couldn't *afford* sugar.

Tales of a-plenty

By all accounts, breakfast in the eighteenth and early nineteenth centuries was gross and alcoholic.

The Duke of Wellington reported that the ailing George IV had breakfasted on beefsteak pie, pigeons, a bottle of Moselle, a glass of champagne, two of port and one of brandy. How the austere Iron Duke must have winced as his fat monarch slurped all this down.

But in the last 100 years part of the pleasure of the well-founded breakfast was not how much you ate but how much was available. It was the subtle art of selection and rejection according to mood and appetite.

I remember, when staying at a house in the Scottish border country that was renowned for having the finest cook in Scotland, the chatelaine came down, hatted and veiled for a shopping expedition to Edinburgh. While the rest of us went through every exquisite dish on the hot plates and the cold table, she breakfasted on artichaut vinaigrette followed by red currants and cream.

A visitor to a *very* millionairish establishment in the 1930s watched fascinated as his host gloomily lifted the lids of the seventeen silver dishes on the hot plates, rejected them all, and summoned a footman to bring him a boiled egg.

In the great Rothschild days of Waddesdon Manor a guest, on being awakened by a man servant, suffered ordeal by catechism.

Man: tea, coffee or chocolate, sir?

Guest: tea, please.

Man: Indian, China or Ceylon?

Guest: Indian.

Man: Milk, cream or lemon?

Guest: Milk.

Man: Jersey, Guernsey or Shorthorn?

Guest: Oh, whatever comes – *and no sugar.*

Three tales of a-plenty going a-begging. In this egalitarian-minded age one can only hope that there were plenty of perks going for the servants: after all, most breakfast dishes do not recycle. The only thing to do with an unused poached egg is to eat it as a poached egg (perhaps, by then, a little leathery), and as the gentry invariably prefer their bacon crisp, left overs could not be the basis of a bacon pie. Profligate it may have been, but enough had to be cooked to fulfil Mrs Beeton's demand for 'substantial' eating by everyone staying in the house.

The cold table, with its meat and fruits, was another matter. Here, gentlemen would carve themselves slices of ham or pheasant to wrap up and put in their pockets to go out hunting, and the peaches and strawberries would be there for luncheon or dinner.

Two sybaritic breakfasts

Oh sensual breakfast! Because the food was already there, one's sense of smell was first to be overwhelmed on entering the room. Smell, the most evocative of the senses. I still drool at the memory of catching the mingled aromas of eggs, bacon, sausages, kidneys, mushrooms and tomatoes, the methylated spirit burners, the fresh fruit, the coffee pots bumbling away, fresh bread and toast and scones, marmalade and jam, and a log fire quietly crackling.

Conversation was low, desultory, trivial. (Many years ago a peppery major in the Brigade of Guards, eating his breakfast alone in the mess was interrupted by a newly joined ensign with a 'Good Morning.'

'Good morning, good morning, good morning, good morning – and that'll do yer for the rest of the week,' barked the major).

A rustle of morning newspapers, the leisurely chumping of jaws, the clink of knives and forks, provided the background to few pleasantries about the weather and secret glances between two pairs of eyes if there had been a spot of illicit bedroom visiting during the night. But positively no discussions about Proust; and the only political comment was your host's barked expletives as he shook the Parliamentary reports in the *Morning Post*.

This utterly pleasant soporific could go on for hours. Energetic early risers would have eaten and gone about their business before those who had drunk late into the night came down to make their first shaky stab at drinking a cup of coffee. As footmen and parlourmaids replenished dishes, the morning sun's increasing warmth reinforced the log fire.

I must tempt you to one last blissful breakfast. The ilex-shaded terrace of an elegant Mediterranean villa before the sun has made the air too hot; fruit juices, crisp rolls and croissants, white butter and morella cherry jam, hot coffee and cool milk. Perfect? Yes; but the perfection of an exquisite watercolour – a petit déjeuner – compared to the baroque splendours of the country house breakfast.

Mrs Beeton was right, but what *would* she say now?

Spring 1978

Drinking in Warm Weather

(including some useful recipes)

Bruce Blunt

The most memorable experiment in hot-weather drinking was carried out by a Cheshire squire in Barcelona, whose idea of returning the hospitality of his many Spanish friends was to regale them during a heat-wave with bowl after steaming bowl of Punch Royal, which is chiefly composed of rum and port in equal parts.

Their carouse was interrupted by the sudden arrival of Trotsky, who had chosen this torrid moment for the swift organisation of a general strike which paralysed the whole of Catalonia.

The respective responsibilities of Deeside and Russia for this disastrous irruption have never been worked out.

One thing alone is certain. A basic rule of hot-weather drinking had been broken. Politics had been allowed to interfere with it. Politics, which engenders heat beneath the collar more quickly than any other form of insult, must be excluded from all such scenes of summer.

The setting and the state of mind must be as refreshing as the drink itself if peace is going to prevail.

The coolest room at home, the shadiest vine-clad arbour of Provence, the greenest stretch of Dordogne, Loire or Rhine are the expressions of a need for completeness which goes deeper than the quenching of a thirst.

The drinks, too, should be as uncontroversial as possible. They should be gay and gracious and suitable for being chilled. We do not want the grand ones which call for argument or for an effort of appreciation or for a nicety of treatment which might cause us to perspire with apprehension before we get them to the glass.

First choice are white and rosé wines, not the dark, heavy rosés of the Rhône Valley, but the rosés of Anjou and Arbois, and that palest *oeil-de-perdrix* rosé of Burgundy which comes from *Marsannay-la-Côte*.

Ice clinks in the imagination against bottles of Champagne, Alsace, Hock, Moselle, Vouvray, Pouilly-Fuissé, Aligoté and Muscadet.

Then there is the wine of Médis. I can only guess at the whereabouts of Médis, and I have never drunk a glass of it in my life, but my reason for recommending it will soon become apparent.

> The painters Corot and Courbet, with their friend Baudry, from Royan, dined copiously off green claires, oysters, sausages, eel stew and fricassée of rabbit, washed down with a small white wine of Médis. In the September moonlight they decided to go for a row on the river. Corot and Courbet rowed and rowed. Baudry took the tiller, and the boat didn't move a yard. The wine of Médis, heavy as the devil, was having its effect. It took them a long time to realise that they had never raised the anchor.

Those small and deceptive white wines can be the enchanters of a summer's night.

High among them I would place Aligoté, that minor white wine of Burgundy which takes its name from the grape which makes it. No wine varies more according to the place from which it comes. The ordinary run of Aligoté from the flatlands is apt to be acid, thin and insignificant. But when it is made from the same grape grown in Savigny, or the Chaume de Narvaux at Meursault, or on the slopes of villages like St Aubin, it acquires a perfume and an elegance which give it the right to dance among the princesses on the starlit lawn.

The delicately witty wines of Alsace – crisp Sylvaner, dry, flowery Riesling and spicy Traminer – seem to blend in themselves the meadow, the vine and the table spread beside the river, and also have the advantage of blending cleanly with other wines.

> A bottle of Champagne and a bottle of Alsatian wine, with lemon-juice and raspberries or wild strawberries make a delightful cup.

Of all red wines which can be chilled without a care, there is nothing to beat a light, fresh Beaujolais – the Beaujolais de Lyon – which is drunk so copiously through the hot days and evenings among its native hills.

Its neighbours, the red and, of course, the white, Mâcons are none the worse for chilling. They are often the better for it. This also applies to Chablis and other lighter wines which can be drunk with great enjoyment when the glass is dim with cold.

Pedantic connoisseurs may detect barbarity in this, but a heat-wave can be a very barbarous thing, and I have never managed to outwit it with a nice civilised cup of tea.

This is not to suggest that wine is the only solution to the problem. Here are some others, though wine is naturally not excluded from them all.

Planter's Punch

The classic proportions are:
    1 of sharp – fresh lemon or lime juice.
    2 of sweet – sugar.
    3 of strong – rum.
    4 of weak – water, ice.
A trifle acid, I think, so that the figure for rum could well be changed to 4. The rum should be Martinique or very light Jamaican.

The Best Mint Julep

Put into a tumbler about six tender shoots of mint, upon this a teaspoonful of white sugar, and equal proportions of peach and ordinary brandy, to fill up one-third of the tumbler. Leave for a few minutes, then fill up with pounded ice, and drink through a straw or a stick of macaroni.

George Roberts's White Wine Cup

Put into a glass jug some slices of lemon and orange and any other fruit to hand, such as a few whole strawberries, quartered peach, etc.; a sprig of borage and some cucumber rind. Leave to infuse with half-gill brandy and half-gill curaçao. When required, add ice, and pour over a bottle of dry white wine or champagne, and a pint of soda water.

Claret Cup

Peel of one lemon, finely cut, covered with sugar. Pour over a glass of sherry, add ice, a bottle of claret, a sprig of vermouth and a bottle of soda water.

Port Wine Cup

A bottle of port and a bottle of red Bordeaux. A few blackcurrant tips steeped in the port till they just impart a flavour, together with a few other herbs to taste. Strain, add the Bordeaux, and ice; sweeten to taste, and add 1-2 pints of soda water.

Summer Favourite

Into a large glass goblet put a quartered peach, and pour over it chilled Moselle, hock or champagne.

Vin Blanc Cassis

Into a good-sized wineglass pour a tablespoonful or more of Crème de Cassis and fill up with Aligoté, Meursault or other dry white Burgundy. The colour of this peerless apéritif can vary from pale pink to ruby according to taste.

These drinks are not guaranteed to reduce your temperature to clinical coolness. They are meant to keep you happy in the sun.

Summer 1957

Muffins and Crumpets

'I have a breakfast of philosophers tomorrow at ten punctually. Muffins and metaphysics, crumpets and contradiction. Will you come?' – *Sydney Smith to Thomas Moore*.

Anon

It's true that, in the countryside, muffins or crumpets are still served – lashed with butter and bramble jelly – to those returning for tea after a day's shooting, hunting, racing or, even, golf. But who today could face up to crumpets for breakfast?

To comprehend the gargantuan capacity for food in Sydney Smith's time, we need only turn to one of his letters to the Countess of Grey who was, apparently, a trifle out of sorts. He writes from Edinburgh, 1829:

> Dr Thomson advises as follows for you:
> Broiled meat at breakfast, an egg, and chocolate.
> At twelve a basin of rich soup.
> At two, a meat luncheon and a tumbler of porter.
> A jelly at four.
> Dinner at six; four or five glasses of claret.
> Tea and a whole muffin.
> Hot supper and negus at ten.
> Something nourishing at the side of your bed.

Co-founder of the *Edinburgh Review*, wit, essayist, farmer, gourmet and gourmand, Sydney Smith took Anglican Orders to placate his father. First, vicar of Foston, with the benefice of Londesborough in Yorkshire, he was translated to a prebend of Bristol Cathedral and the living of Combe Florey (shades of Evelyn Waugh!) and was finally topped-up with a Canonry of St Paul's. He was ever welcome in the top Whig circle of Holland House, and accumulated a vast number of devoted friends. Here he writes to Lady Holland.

> I take the liberty to send you two brace of grouse – curious, because killed by a Scotch metaphysician; in other and better language they are mere ideas, shot by other ideas, out of a purely intellectual notion called a gun.

Writing again to Lady Holland, he sends a rhymed recipe for salad:

> Let onion atoms lurk within the bowl
>   And, half-suspected, animate the whole.
>
> Serenely full, the epicure would say,
>   'Fate cannot harm me, I have dined today.'

We now call on Old Compton to give us a couple of recipes:

From Good Cookery by Mrs W.G.R. Francillon, J.M. Dent, 1920:

Muffins: $\frac{3}{4}$ lb flour (warmed): $\frac{1}{4}$ pint milk; $\frac{1}{2}$ oz yeast (creamed) with teas; sugar; 1 egg; 1 oz butter; 1 oz sugar, pinch of salt.

Melt butter, add milk, and when blood heat mix to the yeast. Add it by degrees to flour and sugar, together with beaten egg. Beat to a light dough. Divide into 4 or 6 flat round cakes. Knead each slightly and put in greased and floured tin. Prick with fork and set to rise. When dough rises to top of tin, bake in moderate oven 20 mins. Cut in half, toasted and buttered.

Crumpets or Pikelets: 1 lb flour (warmed); 1 pint milk; 2 teaspoons salt; 2 oz yeast; 2 eggs; 2 oz butter:

Cream the yeast and salt. To this add $\frac{1}{4}$ pint warm water. Make a sponge with this and part of the flour. Set to rise. Add the melted butter and warmed milk, and gradually mix in the rest of the flour, adding the beaten eggs. Beat well. Set to rise for about 2 hours. Grease a girdle and some crumpet rings. Pour half a cup of the batter into each ring. When sufficiently cooked and firm enough, remove the rings and turn the crumpets to cook on the other side. The girdle must not be too hot, or the crumpets will burn before they have finished rising.

Autumn/Winter 1976

The Male-Chauvinist Muffin

Robin Baillie

Said the Muffin to the Crumpet,*
'I would really like to know
If each of us was different,
When both of us were dough.'

'A Cook begot us in a bowl
From water mixed with flour
Quite forgot we had a Soul,
And baked us for an hour,
In an oven at a temperature
I'm fearful to relate,
Poked us with a metal skewer,
And threw us on a plate.'

'Yet now we are as different,
As two peas so unalike
That one of us is masculine
And the other, well – ladylike.'

'Now that I have had my say,
I'll join the Muffineers†,
And you can stay at home all day
And dry your greasy tears.'

* Thanks to the advent of the Sixth Edition of the *Concise Oxford Dictionary*, edited with rare enlightenment by J.B. Sykes, *Oxford at the Clarendon Press*, £4.75, the definition of **crumpet** is no longer restricted to a trite culinary reference, but now adds, if tardily: (sl.) sexually desirable woman, women collectively (17th c., of uncert. orig.).

† Castor for sprinkling salt or sugar on muffins: Georgian silver models now eagerly in demand.

Autumn/Winter 1976

Music at Mealtimes

Spike Hughes

The practice of eating to the sound of music is undoubtedly of considerable antiquity, for Izaak Walton credits the Romans, 'at the height of their glory', with ushering in their dishes of lamprey, sturgeon and mullet with music. How or why this ancient habit started nobody knows for certain; music, we have been told, may be the food of love, but there has never been any suggestion that in consequence food should involve love of music.

And yet Pepys was constantly complaining that he expected 'musique, the missing of which spoiled my dinner'.

* * *

In spite of the ubiquitousness of mealtime music, Austria – land of Schoenberg, Webern and Berg – is by no means top of the league when it comes to the provision of music on a grand scale to eat to. This particular championship is indisputably held by the Italians. On a Venetian summer night you may sit in the Piazza and eat to the sound of music coming from your café, the café on your right, the café on your left, and from the admirable Italian naval band in the middle of the square playing the Enigma Variations as a compliment to the visiting Mediterranean Fleet, whose personnel is elsewhere in Venice searching for eggs on chips to eat to the accompaniment of mealtime music provided by television and juke-box.

Florence, besides being the most beautiful of cities is also the noisiest, and features what must surely be the loudest form of mealtime music known to man: a soprano and a tenor who regale with operatic duets all within earshot of the city's largest café. I use the word 'regale' advisedly, for it derives from the Italian 'regalo' – a gift. And while the customers for whom this entertainment is immediately intended pay through the nose for it, the volume of the performance is such that it can be heard above the Vespas and may be enjoyed free of charge in otherwise music-less restaurants a couple of blocks away, as well as by several hundred Florentines who just stand around in the street and listen.

But it is Naples, with its centuries-old tradition of popular music and its equally old and highly organised begging system, which is unsurpassed in the practice of inflicting music at mealtimes. At no time of day, in no kind of weather, and in no class of restaurant, is there more than a moment's respite from the wandering musician: violinist, singer, guitarist, accordionist – they come endlessly, singly and together. And there is no escape, no refuge round the corner which they or some other band of conspiring virtuosi will not invade in a few minutes' time.

The student of 'folclor' may think that the disturbance of his Neapolitan meal will at least be compensated for by hearing the traditional popular music of Naples at close quarters in authentic surroundings and in authentic performance. He will be lucky if it is. The last time I was there the most popular selection was the late Jerome Kern's 'Smoke Gets in Your Eyes', a catchpenny idea inspired by the apparently permanent presence in the city of the entire US Navy and played in a way that resulted in a most intriguing form of Alien Corn.

But mealtime music can have its points, and indeed can be instructive as well as entertaining. I remember a meal in Vienna during which the orchestra played the Intermezzo from Mascagni's Cavalleria Rusticana – conducted by the composer, who took his bow and returned to his dinner. On the whole, however, I think Mozart had the right idea. At the end of Don Giovanni, where he is swallowed up in Hell Fire, it is generally supposed that Don Juan is being punished for killing the Commendatore. It isn't. It is because he ordered music for the dinner to which he invited the Statue. It was Mozart's revenge for having had to write more mealtime music to be eaten and talked through than any other composer in history.

Sweets

Old Compton's Fancy, January

Old Compton's friends know him as a man of almost superhuman goodwill, whose kindness and generosity radiate from him like an aura, and whose outward appearances confirm these qualities not only by the warmth and love in his eye but also by the peculiar curvature of his spine, caused by years of bending over backwards in his efforts to speak and write and think only good of his neighbours.

Particularly does Old Compton feel for his fellow-hacks, appreciating as he does the toil they perform and the anguish they suffer till each last polished phrase is set down, till each pregnant sentence is curetted by the editor's pencil. And even then, as if all this were not enough, there is the critic's sterile knife and the reader's general unwillingness to buy his book unless it be remaindered, or specially reduced, or paper-backed, or, in a field in which Old Compton has not planted wild oats, condemned as obscene.

Nevertheless the milk of Old Compton's kindness occasionally sours, and after having read (more truthfully 'ploughed through') Nell Heaton's *Puddings* (Arco Press, 15s.), his charity will allow him only to describe it as ranking high amongst the more pedestrian books he has had to tackle.

In violent reaction from *Puddings* Old Compton begs to offer a suggestion for a wildly extravagant dessert.

Take as many fresh strawberries as the host can afford (at this time of the year in England they will have come from Kenya, California or from the hot-house), cut a triangular cone from each which includes the stalk. Arrange the strawberries in a dish so that they stand upright, and pour a little Green Chartreuse into each. Leave in a cool place until the fruit has closed itself over the liqueur, an hour or so. Eat.

Spring 1959

191

Meals to Remember

Lord St Oswald

Of the 'insular and effete' English aristocracy, Rowland Winn, 4th Baron St Oswald, MC, had a Polish wife and a Spanish cook. Educated Stowe, Bonn and Freiburg. Contrived by the age of twenty to be sentenced to death, spent eleven days in the Condemned Cell while a Press correspondent in Spain. Commissioned, 8th Hussars, he served in the Western Desert and in 1944 was parachuted behind the Japanese forces into Siam, and also fought in French Indo-China. Rejoined his regiment in Korea, 1950; awarded MC and Belgian Order of Leopold and Croix de Guerre.

Latterly an assiduous Parliamentarian.

During the forty odd years since I became critically aware of my palate, I have held in principle to the straight and narrow path between epicurism and pure greed. But on occasion, Bacchus be praised, I have tip-toed off delicately and expensively to the right, and in other instances trampled away exuberantly to the left. Not being a collector of menu cards, the log of such joyous and generally impromptu excursions was never kept. And, excepting a few cases, memory has tended to preserve the effect, the general gratification of the hour, while discarding the detail.

* * *

In an earlier article of this series, Patrick Kinross paid a handsome compliment to my cook, Rosario, who comes from Spain. We discovered her there, and brought her to Yorkshire, for the good of our household and our guests. In the matter of her activities, I have not been backward with encouragement and advice. Happily she responds to both. Some of these dishes were served to the Prime Minister on a recent week-end visit to Nostell: Huevos a la Mimosa – Soufflé de Pescado – Pichones en Cazuela con lentejas; Crêpes Rosario – Mousse aux Framboises – and, as one would assume, *Paella Valenciana*. It is Rosario's claim that this most celebrated of Spanish dishes can be better composed in the British Isles than in its native Iberia – the chickens being that much plumper and more succulent here.

* * *

From the Albanian campaign of 1944, I can still recapture, with poignant precision, the flavour of every sheep's eye which diplomacy forced me to consume. I still prefer oysters. There is something about the whole roast sheep itself, served up after sixty hours of sleepless battle, which returns more pleasantly to the sense, with a moment or two of concentration.

But food is not the most enticing aspect of life in the Balkans as a whole (excepting, that is, *cevapcice*, grilled under the stars, over a primitive charcoal brazier, its fragrance infusing the bland Illyrian dusk.)

* * *

The most extravagant eating I have done has been in the Orient. But again, the panorama of Chinese cooking tends to defeat memory, overwhelming and obscuring the wonderful, wasteful details, except here and there. You can't see the nests for the birds. I revere it as the superlative in human food, when it is eaten *in situ* – that is to say when circumstances have shipped you somewhere East of Suez by above 2,000 miles. The same dishes served in Europe have never done more than tantalise my palate with a recollection of the real thing.

Ritual is, of course, very much a part of the gratification. At tactful stages, possibly only at half-time and at the end of the meal, there is one exact service that a man requires – it is that a delicate, smiling Chinese maiden should glide up behind him, and with deft, solicitous hands apply a cool, damp cloth to his face, to remove the light beading of perspiration which the enjoyment of the meal has cost. In the performance of this altogether charming service, she will smile at you out of black, sparkling eyes, under a smooth crown of hair – black as plutonium, black as the hard-boiled eggs two hundred years old, with which you began the meal.

* * *

But undoubtedly the best-remembered meal I was offered in the East, was on the left bank of the Mekong River, with three Chinese Generals. The senior officer (in culinary rank, at least – their relative army status remained a secret to me throughout) was General Tso-tsi Peng. He provided two delicacies, both of which had been brought, I believe, very nearly 1,000 miles, the last stage by fast rowers, taking advantage of the current. We lunched in a level clearing in the jungle, and first a tall silver jar was placed, with some ceremony, before my host. When he raised the lid, a small monkey popped its head above the rim. The General caught up a knife from the ground beside him, and in a single neat stroke removed the top of the monkey's skull. It was essential, the interpreter explained, that we should eat its brains while they were still warm.

Ten days after writing this, I shall be in New Orleans, on my first visit to America. Friends who have been to New Orleans speak, with misty eyes, about the food. They murmur longingly about soft-shelled crabs and Pampano en Papillotte. Another summit beyond another sea I shall keep the flag flying as best I can.

Autumn 1958

Meals to Remember

including some delicious rencontres with late Victorian personalities ...

Sir Shane Leslie

Eton, King's College, Cambridge and LL.D. Notre Dame University, USA; author and professor. Wrote verse and biography which ranged from *Epic of Jutland* to *Life of Mrs Fitzherbert* and *From Cabin Boy to Archbishop*. To say nothing of a haunting *Ghost Book*. Deeply interested in Irish archaeology – and forestry. Shared with Sir Winston Churchill the same maternal grandfather – Leonard Jerome of New York.

I am not a gourmet; I remember meals not for wine but wits. Like Swift I have said to hostesses: Show me your list of guests, not your courses.

*   *   *

Nobody today knows what level leisurely good conversation is. But it was built up on choice foods and even choice wines.

The Victorian dinner of six courses and three wines served by flunkeys under a whiskered butler put men into fettle. The men gave the heavily dressed and jewelled ladies their small talk but to men they talked as men afterwards.

My most enduring memories are of Professor Mahaffy (later Provost of Trinity, Dublin) after the Claret had satisfied him at dinner and the Port had proved its vintage. He could then talk for an hour or more – Greek adventures, cricket in the Phoenix Park (between the murders), kings and queens he had met, the brothels of the ancients (Roman and Greek), how to shoot snipe on Irish bogs, how to cook woodcock (fresh trail in a bird shot a week previously), how he had trained Oscar Wilde in Dublin in Greek, in conversation and knowledge of wine – all this information was spliced by anecdotes in cleancut sentences.

Mahaffy once stopped the wine at a Cambridge College because they were fobbing off a Red Sauterne as Claret. He made them send for their Founders Day beverage – and they obeyed!

Another type of Irish talker was Derry Rossmore. He and his brother came straight out of a Lever novel. The elder rode in the last moonlighted-nightshirt steeplechase across country (like the famous series of prints). He was the love of —, the best-looking courtesan in England, and was killed at a jump on Windsor racecourse in front of Queen Victoria's carriage. He treated Her Majesty to some 'Queen's English' before dying which warned her off the turf for ever. His brother succeeded to the peerage and lasted till the 1920s. He had a saga of brilliantly told, heavily brogued stories – lasting two hours – which for sheer delight saved many a young man straying off to a bagnio.

It was the same with the three Beresford brothers who were unfailing in singles or trios.

They were Lord Charles the Admiral, Lord Bill the VC, and Lord Marcus the king's trainer.

Lord Charles was the boy-friend of Lady —. When Lady Charles had a baby, Lady — wrote accusing him of infidelity to herself. Alas, Lady Charles opened the letter!

Lord Bill brought Tod Sloan, the American jockey to England, married a duchess, left dead Zulus in Africa and swooning ladies in India, where he was Military Secretary to three Viceroys.

Lord Marcus was the wit who gave King Edward VII two Derby winners. When Ernest Cassel wanted to put his KCMG on his horsebox, Marcus told him to put the 'Gee' inside.

Once, two of the brothers tricked the third into jumping into bed at a country house party between a bishop and his wife. They had changed the door numbers, pretended a Prima Donna expected him and warned him that no light should be turned up.

They had the power to bring the shocks of Irish conversation into the dullest English parties.

Autumn 1956

A Touch of the
Tarte Aux Prunes

yet another mishap midst the tranquillity of Charente Maritime

Stuart Ross

The Atlantic coastline of Charente Maritime runs from just above the impressive medieval port of La Rochelle, south for eighty kilometres to the mouth of the gigantic Gironde estuary. In the lee of the offshore Ile d'Oleron the sheltered waters provide an abundance throughout the year of mussels and oysters. A feature in the estuary is the 'carralet' – a large square fishing net raised and lowered by a mechanism housed in a little wooden hut often perched precariously on cliff edges. I have not seen their like in other countries. The carralets provide us with those most succulent small shrimps, crevette grise. A handful are just right – with a glass of champagne or mousseux and are a welcome relief from the monotony of tea and cake.

However, I suppose it's because we are English that periodically we get invited 'to tea'.

I have never been mad about this gastronomic intrusion between lunch and dinner and it is a ceremony with which I can well dispense. Here as a foreigner one is in duty bound to extol the virtues of some hideously sticky gâteau only to find another great wedge plonked on your plate. By the time three cups of tea have been consumed the thought of dinner is a nauseating improbability.

Unfortunately I have learned from experience that the tea and gâteaux are but 'round one' in the battering. This is hastily followed by a glass of white Bordeaux wine and a tarte aux prunes which, round in shape, stares one straight in the eye with a sickly smirk. To jib at round two is not only impolite but invites a further sickening wallop of round one.

The French with irritating vivacity seem expert at coping with this terrifying intake whilst at the same time carrying on a voluble and animated conversation on subjects ranging from the merits of Molière to the price of oysters.

I drift into a comatose haze leaving Madame to represent the Raj. My mind feels sluggish and the working parts, gummed by gâteau, find difficulty in assimilating the conversation. My eyes take on the viscous glaze of a glutinous tarte aux pommes.

When the Garriolas invited us for tea I knew we were in for a blockbuster. A giant of a man, my host was one of those truly international characters with a fluent command of half a dozen languages. Born of an Italian father and a French mother, his father's mother was English and his maternal grandmother Egyptian. He was raised by a German nanny in Athens where he went to school.

We had tea in the conservatory. The opening round was strawberries and cream.

'Today, dah boy, we are all terribly English' he thundered as we waded gamely into round two – a particularly rich and melliferous chocolate cake.

Sure enough it was to be a three-rounder. The dreaded tarte aux prunes stared up at me. I was considering devious ways of passing on my portion to the dog who was sniffing my right trouser leg when I became aware that my host was in trouble. His huge frame had stiffened in the cane chair opposite me. His eyes stared unseeingly through me and beyond. His face was flushed – his mouth open as though he had been interrupted in the middle of a sentence.

'Lolette,' I said to his wife, who at that moment was more concerned with her second tranche of tarte aux prunes than her husband's health, 'something's wrong with Roby.'

For a big woman she moved with surprising agility. She knelt in front of her husband and spoke in rapid French. Roby's face was now crimson and globules of sweat glinted on his forehead. He gasped a few words in reply. I only caught the word 'stuck' and in a flash I realised the cause of his anguish – one of those ghastly plum stones had got wedged in his windpipe.

'He's got a stone stuck in his throat, Lolette, hasn't he?'

Her reaction was most extraordinary. She laughed and continued laughing uproariously. In fact she couldn't stop. With her face buried in Roby's lap her plumpish frame vibrated with mirth. Poor Roby meanwhile was a shade of scarlet – his mouth further open – his eyes bulbous and frightened.

I was a bewildered onlooker. Obviously he was not seriously ill despite his looks. Lolette, besides her prolific expertise in producing gooey gâteau, was a competent and affectionate wife.

'No! No! it's not a stone that's stuck …' Her laughter overcame her again and she was unable to continue.

'It's too ridiculous,' she recovered herself sufficiently to be serious for a moment, 'poor Roby's *roupettes* have somewhat slipped through the cane slats in the chair – it really is too absurd.'

Absurd or not it was obvious from his expression that that part of his anatomy now suspended between the cane slate was being held there in a vice-like grip which permitted movement only at considerable risk.

'Let's look under the chair, Lolette, and see what's happened.'

A cursory glance was all that was necessary to disclose a nasty and tricky situation. The poor chap's *bijoux de famille* were in grave and imminent danger.

Perhaps because I was more aware than Lolette of the immense pain, both physical and psychological, which was involved I decided to take command of the salvage operations.

'You can see the two slats involved can't you? Separate them at the front and at the same time I will pull them apart at the back. For heaven's sake make sure you have got hold of the right bits of cane or we may do irreparable damage.'

That we had made a wise selection was immediately apparent as Roby's burly frame rocketed upwards like a happily released champagne cork.

'Dah boy', he said from the secure comfort of a Louis Quinze settee, 'I wouldn't give that chair to my worst enemy.'

He stretched forward for another slice of tarte aux prunes. 'Now let's get stuck into something worth while!'

Winter 1981

The Well-Mannered Wedge

By Request

Bruce Blunt

New ideas about cheese have the impact of a major revolution. For most of my life, the silver-plated cheese scoop and the Stilton have seemed to be inseparable, and the crumbling walls about the final crater to be among the noblest ruins of mankind.

I have now reluctantly come to the conclusion that the Stilton cheese makers are right when they recommend that the half-Stilton for home use should be cut in wedges of about knife-blade depth across the surface so that when one layer has been cut off, the top of the cheese remains level, and so on, to the end.

This conclusion has only been reached after the sort of soul-searching which attends a religious conversion, and I hope that the ritual of the scoop will never be abandoned in the restaurant, where the ripe cheese is naturally finished more quickly than at home.

A Stilton keeps well in the larder, wrapped in greaseproof paper. It should be turned every other day so that its moisture can be distributed as evenly as possible.

If it shows signs of dryness, soak a cloth in water, then wring it out, and cover the cheese with this for a few days. Texture and flavour will soon reassert themselves.

Sometimes a Stilton shows hesitancy about developing on one side. In this case cut a shallow v-trench on the surface of the backward side, not far from the rind, and following the curve of it. Pour a little beer occasionally into this trench and you will find that more even development will soon set in. As a half-Stilton weighs about 7 lb and half of a Blue Wensleydale even less, the foregoing remarks apply equally to both of them.

When it comes to the other great English cheeses, Cheddar, Cheshire, Blue Cheshire, Double Gloucester and Leicester, we are dealing with cheeses which weigh from 80 lb to 40 lb, so we naturally do not buy them by the half-cheese. We usually buy them in wedges of 2-3 lb. From whatever sort of cheese they may come, these wedges want watching. Each one must be treated on its merits.

For a well-behaved wedge, I do not think that there is any better covering than greaseproof paper. If dryness sets in, a temporary application of a damp cloth, as recommended for Stilton, usually does the trick.

Never keep any sort of cheese in captivity beneath the cover of a cheese-dish. For serving cheese at table these dishes can be decorative, but as permanent homes they are stifling and impossible.

Winter 1955

After the Turkey Bird

(with hints for the wise purchaser)

Alec Blacke

The turkey-bird's come and gone, its first pristine rotundity, like the better curves of a well-corseted Gaiety girl, now reduced to the meagre proportions of a contemporary filleted fashion model; the attendant stuffing, savoury as that Edwardian chorine's repartee, lies coagulating on the plates, cold and dead.

Even the sprouts, vital attendants on the bird, have suffered a sea-change ... they came, smoking hot, as green as the eyes of a respectable housewife looking at a demi-monde's mink coat, and as hard and as small and as crisp as a grape fresh-picked from the vine. For your lady abjured the soggy miniature footballs on which England's greatness was built, and paved the way to heaven knows what further continental excesses by buying the elegant Choux de Bruxelles instead, and cooking them briefly and gently with the sweetest of chestnuts. There must be no false patriotism about these either, for our native nuts, alas, are fit only for feeding to the pigs; the largest and plumpest and dirtiest-looking Naples chestnuts only, and you may boil them or glaze them or roast them round the fire without fear of finding an unwelcome wiggly visitor wishing you a Merry Christmas as you bite one open.

* * *

A Woman, a Dog ...

So the bird has gone, and the pudding, too ... *eheu fugaces* ... but some of the best is yet to come. On every hand are boxes and drums and little silver dishes. Fine walnuts, looking as if they were carved from the palest of boxwood, from France and Italy ... or, with great wealth, you may have the giant English double walnuts, dirty-looking and succulent ... and will you be able to resist, given enough port, saying with great solemnity, 'A woman, a dog, and a walnut tree; the more you beat 'em the better they be,' looking meaningly at your wife, so that the children scream in terror, and the women giggle at some primitive recollection from their subconscious ... perhaps you will, perhaps you will.

Treasure trove

Then there must be Brazil nuts, gathered for you 1,000 miles up the Amazon, the great polished shells from Mañaos, or the smaller but no less succulent Toccattin variety; great merit may be acquired by being able to crack nut after nut so that the kernel emerges whole, the secret being to crack each end first, and then the middle. And Spanish filberts, and Valencia almonds, for which seek out only those that have flaky shells; if you succumb to the brighter-looking husks, you will need to call in a pile-driver to crack them.

Sated with nuts, the idle fingers pause, then move again. Shall they alight on a box of sticky dates, hight by the Arabs *Deglet Nour* – 'Fingers of the Light'? Just one or two, perhaps, but they must be from Tunis, and must have not more than the Cabbalistic number thirteen in the top layer. There's a dish of sugared plums of Carlsbad, and another of syrupy Elvas plums; a box of French marrons, far too good for the children, and candied apricots too rich for diet-conscious waistlines, better leave those all for Father!

Cornucopian prospect

No more? But there's more, and still more to come; the whole world waits to pour out its delicacies for you upon this Christmas Day! Take a clementine, red-skinned, seedless, and ready to lave with its scented juice the most sugar-sated tongue ... or the more pungent mandarine, paler, loose-skinned, but perhaps more reminiscent of Christmas than its more sophisticated cousin; both from Sicily, I think, although the Spanish and the Israeli too have their adherents.

And the pineapple, that's stood solid-bottomed in its place throughout the meal, its scent filling the air ... at least it should, if it be so ripe that the leafy crown will twist in the hand, or a leaf pull away freely when held in two fingers. From the pale dwarf from the Cape, to the Red Spanish that hails from Jamaica and Cuba; from the almost first-rate Kenya pineapple that was born in Kew Gardens, and sent out to Africa as a colonist, the noble shapely prince of Pineapples that grows only in St Michael in the Azores ... according to your purse, so shall ye know them ... don't fiddle-faddle with rich cream, or sherry, or any of the other titivations prescribed by the food-torturers of the women's magazines, but cut a fair slice, and manfully endure the astringency for the sake of the sweetness that follows.

Perfect ending

And so dinner draws to its close, this dinner of all dinners of the year, dallying with a fresh fig if only for the sake of its black skin and brilliant scarlet flesh, like a negress' smile, and perhaps a Kaki ... persimmon to the Anglo-Saxon ... that looks like a golden tomato and, ripe enough, tastes as sweet as one of the more interesting sins. To finish, to clear the palate, to settle the stomach ... if settled it can be ...

and because it's vastly different from anything that came before, a superlative English Cox's Orange Pippin, russeted, pip-rattling, sweetly tart, green and red like the Kent or Essex autumn countryside that saw it picked ... and a goodly wedge of English cheese, Cheshire or Cheddar, to give it body.

That eaten, the time is come when *paterfamilias* may sleep a little in his chair, and the hostess, fair but fatiguée (and all the assortment of female relatives) can cope with the washing-up, and the children, 'quietly, quietly', at last can slaughter each other with Atomic Ray Guns and Wild Bill Colts ... the perfect ending to a Christmas dinner, British style, any year.

Winter 1958

'*Whadsamada, Honey?*'

Michael Watkins

A waitress called Jane made that particular day for me. She works in Lucerne Valley which, as everyone knows, is not far from Dead Man Point in the Mojave Desert. 'Welcome to Lucerne Valley. Pop 50' read the sign at the edge of the town where tumbleweed swirled like loose balls of knitting across the dust. 'Town' is not entirely apt: there was a smart caravan with 'Bank of America' emblazoned on its side, a gas station, a store of sorts, and Filippi's Country Kitchen where Jane waits table.

She was fortyish and roundly pneumatic. Her hair was burnished candy floss: each tortured curl having its established place in the order of the universe. Her even teeth gleamed a fluoride gleam of regular brushing. She was obvious, loud, persistent. She had, I suspect, not an enemy in the world.

'Whadsamada, honey?' she demanded as I left a sandwich crust built like Hadrian's Wall. 'You don't like it?' I must try, she insisted, the apple-pie *à la mode*. She had made it herself. And when I came to pay the bill I saw she hadn't charged for the apple-pie.

Winter 1981

Rum in the Kitchen

Olive Dawes

Until about a generation ago, rum was considered a rather 'Non-Mitford' drink, and thought of rather in terms of 'Yo-ho-ho', grog, and perhaps an occasional hot toddy to keep the cold out. Not so now: in fact, in a rapidly increasing number of households, rum has taken its place as a 'must' in the wine cellar and, being *there* and available, should be made use of in the kitchen also – and in the following ways:

Babas-au-Rhum

Make them at home, of course, but for a last-minute dinner party, when there isn't time to prepare a sweet oneself, those delectable (though figure-destroying!) Babas-au-Rhum, purchased from a reliable patisserie, and given a generous topping-up with rum, make a deliciously rich finale to any meal. There are, of course, almost as many varieties of rum as there are West Indian Islands, ranging in colour from deepest mahogany to purest white. For Babas, the connoisseur would, of course, choose Rhum (with an 'h') from the French islands of Guadeloupe or Martinique. This is not easy to come by; for you or me, one of the dark, heavy-bodied rums, say, from Jamaica, would serve the purpose equally well, though any type available would successfully give that extra fillip that makes all the difference. For general use in the kitchen, Barbados Rum is particularly recommended. It is a clear, smooth, finely-distilled 'brandy' type rum, light amber in colour, and with less than no aromatic bouquet, which makes it a good mixer, and which, to the aroma-prejudiced, is a recommendation in itself.

Banana Flambé

This is a delicious pudding, with added eye-appeal. Cooking brings out the flavour of bananas to a quite remarkable extent.

Ingredients:

6 large bananas

2 ozs soft brown sugar

$1\frac{1}{2}$ tsps lemon juice

$\frac{3}{4}$ oz butter

1 liqueur glass Barbados Rum

Lightly butter a casserole (8-inch square). Place in the bottom 2 peeled bananas sliced lengthwise into 3. Sprinkle over them $\frac{1}{2}$ oz sugar and $\frac{1}{2}$ teaspoonful of lemon juice. Repeat this layer. Top with remaining sugar and lemon juice and dot with butter. Cover and bake in a moderate oven (Reg. 4) for 30 minutes. **To serve:** Bring to the table, uncover and over the bananas pour the rum; set it alight and serve immediately.

Bananas Baked in their Skins

Choose a ripe banana for each person, lightly prick with a fork and place on a greased baking tray in a moderate oven for about 30 minutes. The skin will have turned black, but do not let this put you off. **To serve:** Slit banana lengthwise, and serve in its skin with soft brown sugar, lemon juice and Rum to taste.

Melon Cocktail

Fill sundae glasses with small melon balls or cubes, flavoured with equal parts of rum and falernum*; sprinkle with ground ginger, and top with a star of preserved ginger.

Barbados Grapefruit Sundae

Cut out the fruit from a halved grapefruit or shaddock (this is similar to a grapefruit, but with pink flesh), cut into segments and remove pith. Peel and stone 6 large black grapes. Fill grapefruit halves with grapefruit segments and grapes: add about 1½ tsps (or to taste) of falernum, and decorate with sliced pistachio nuts and a cherry. No sugar will be required.

Caribbean Crêpes Suzettes

Service thin crêpes with two parts **un**sweetened orange juice to one part Falernum, topped with slices of fresh **green** limes.

Mount Gay Apricots

Ingredients:
　1 lb dried apricots
　Escoffier Sauce Melba
　Tsp powdered gelatine
　Whites of three eggs
　1 tbls Mount Gay Barbados Rum
　Desertspoonful Falernum
Soak apricots overnight, stew with very little water, and purée. Place in a fireproof dish, blend in melted gelatine, rum and falernum; cover thinly with Sauce Melba. Top with stiffly beaten white of egg, and put under grill or in oven to brown.

---

* Falernum: A by-product of Barbados Rum, falernum is a distilled sugar syrup (30% proof), flavoured with almonds, the juice of freshly crushed limes and the essences of Barbados herbs and flowers. It is exclusive to Barbados, having been evolved in the island some 200 years ago. It was found to take the 'heat' out of the rather crude rum ('Kill Divil') of those days, and mixed with it, gave it a smoother passage down the throat! Now available at Fortnum and Mason's, Selfridges and Barkers.

Summer 1963

Wheeleeta

She ate grapes; I would make her drink them –

William Younger

The name has romance, Wheelee-ta! It has the far-off, dreamy music of sea-birds in the pine-trees of Venezia. Whee-lee-ta! It is a seductive name. If she had been called Herthberga, she would not have been so attractive. Or would she? Yes, she would. A maenadet is always a maenadet.

It was not, of course, her name which attracted me at first; it was her manner of eating a Dream-master ice-cream. The method was the same as that of all those unwrinkled girls in their wrinkled jeans – jeanettes, she told me they were, and that has romance, too, jeanettes! A flash of blue jeans in the depth of The Perilous Wood! Ho, Bacchus-Bacchus!

But, as I was saying, it was not her method which attracted me, it was her manner. Her method was to pick with the tip of her spoon at the frosted spiral of the Dream-master: a cherry, a nut, and strawberry ice-cream; an olive, a banana, and chocolate ice-cream; then a cherry, a nut, and a touch of vanilla. There is music in that – 'a cherry, a nut, and a touch of vanilla' – the music of the old-fashioned waltz which they used to play at Hammerfest when I was a boy before the first world war.

No, it was not her method which attracted me; not even that exciting pause when she scratched her ear with the tip of her spoon. It was her manner. She ate her Dream-master with a fierce innocence. No one eats ice-cream with innocence. It is not innocent food. But she did. Oh, my Wheeleeta, my rare discovery, you become vanilla in my veins. I resolved to seduce you to wine.

I acted at once. Not for me the old motto of 'always put off till tomorrow what you cannot get anyone to do for you today.' No, no. Ho, Bacchus-Bacchus! Nothing venture, nothing win. I made the approach. I bought her another ice-cream. She was sick.

I was patient with her. Long years in lodgings in Bergen-op-Zoom had taught me the extremes of patience; they had also hardened my will, tempering it in a changeless eternity of Bismarck Herring. What could she do against this passion of patience and will? Nothing. She was doomed before she had finished being sick.

But — and you may know this too, O gentle reader who would not harm a fly while anyone is looking — the fine art of seduction is that it should be slow. Speed is greed. One must prolong the transmutation of innocence into knowledge. That, to the seducer, is the whole joy. To see the bright, flat, child-world changing and becoming deeper, to see dreams walking in daylight and the panthers snarl behind the candy and the walnut-whip, to see the *fleurs du mal* becoming radiant behind the paper roses in the Milk Bar — to watch those vistas opening in the mind of the seducee, this is the joy of the researching seducer. Through her eyes I should see again wine glowing like magic amber as it glowed for me when I was a student at Bishopsteignton. Then also behind her grubby face would rise the radiance of my first Pernod at Dieppe.

Consider this. She was made, my Wheeleeta, of sugar, soft drinks, and mineral water. She was unknown to alcohol. Hock was a thing a horse had four of. Bordeaux was a place there was once a Richard of. And she *ate* grapes. I would make her drink them. This was my seduction. I began wrong.

The mistake must have been due to an early experience of mine in a suburban train outside Klosterkindergarten. Then a bottle of Moselle had been like spring morning over the cows on the Niedaralp. I remembered its light delicacy (dancing shoes compared to boots), and the pale fragrance of its unbourgeois beauty. This, I thought, would be the opposite to all she had known, the first vision of the difference between vanilla and Mozart. And being a shock, a pale-gold fragrant shock, it would start her irretrievably on the slope from Cola to Château La Tour.

But no. But not at all. The wine from Wehlen was too fine for her. The flowers of its bouquet were too faint for her. She had only until now smelt scents that were harsh by comparison with the bouquet of wine. My error lay in the delicacy. It was too subtle and civilised, and, after the years of the Dream-master ices, the body of the wine was too thin. Her taste fell through it.

So. One must play from strength. One must support her taste with a robust generosity, a wine as robust and generous as the appetite of the young. She must be treated as a fly-eating orchid that was being trained to eat truffled turkey.

I have always theorised that to a boy you give Burgundy. It should be his first wine. It has, it has immediately, the full meaning of wine, the fruit, the fullness, and the song. It is, as my old tutor at Bishopsteignton once put it, Alcohol into Opera. If from his beginning with Burgundy a boy does not begin to love wine, he will never begin. Let Wheeleeta begin like a boy.

It was a Nuits, a great Nuits, a sunburst of dark splendour from the Côte d'Or. It was an embrace in a big glass. She drank some and choked.

I thought back to Bergen-op-Zoom and my patience remained flawless. It was not unreasonable that she should choke. One's first big embrace should be choking. But the second should exhilarate. Then the third – and the next ten thousand – should be necessary to keep one from the cold. Let us try the second.

It burns, she said, it burns, it's the same medicine Nanny used to give me. This latter statement, unless Nanny was unique, was undoubtedly untrue. But the first statement was true; it was the cry of the innocent palate; to the alcohol-innocent alcohol burns. It is the dry, hard impact of the adult life.

And with her cry began the counter-seduction. She was now seducing me, for now I saw through her eyes. Her child's world was opening and, although I could see the long road ahead, yet altogether we trod the first sweet setting-out.

And sweet it was. She ordered steak-and-kidney pudding, and cabbage, and potatoes mashed and roast. And seeing with the eyes of her sugar-youth, I understood at last and ordered a Sauternes, golden and rich and sweet. She drank it with her steak-and-kidney, she drank it with her whole enjoyment and I knew that she was won. She had taken the decisive step beyond the delirious innocence of bubble-gum.

Youth is sweet and so is its taste. It is the basic taste of the world. From that point begins the knowledge of wine. And when we next dined, my Wheeleeta and I – but that is another story.

Spring 1961

In Search of the Obscure

Spike Hughes

Spike Hughes, a leading musician and music critic of his day, famous for broadcasts and for books as diverse as *Great Opera Houses*, *Glyndebourne* and *The Art of Coarse Cricket* was a long-serving, wide-ranging contributor to *Wheeler's Review*. Here are extracts from his series 'Motoring in France', 'Eating for Money' and 'In Search of the Obscure'.

Waiter Extraordinary

Though it lacked the long communal table which is the characteristic feature of the traditional trattoria, the Antico Fattore was friendly and intimate, and neither displayed outside, nor offered inside, any written menu. You listened to what the shirt-sleeved waiter called Marcello recommended, and ordered that.

Marcello was, of course, the son of the house. He was also Professor of Greek at the University of Florence, and his parents had occasionally to enrol his wife as deputy when his academic duties took him away for a couple of nights to lecture in Basel or Vienna. The Vanucci family – Marcello, father and mother – ran the whole concern with the help of one little old man who fanned the charcoal fire and washed up, and had a medieval Florentine face which came straight off the Ghiberti doors of the Baptistery.

In addition to its excellent and cheap Florentine specialities (Marcello's papa made a superb sauce for the tagliatelle, and the roast veal was always a treat), the Antico Fattore introduced us to the delights of finocchiona casalinga – the home-made salami flavoured with fennel that Marcello used to fetch once a week from some tiny unspecified village in the Tuscan countryside. One or two of the older Italian stores in Soho still sometimes have casalinga salami to sell, but not very often and there isn't very much of it.

Spring 1969

To say Van Gogh cut off his ear to spite his face is all just typical artistic overstatement. He didn't cut it off, it was bitten off by the mosquitoes of Arles. They are the size of wasps, and relieved (it is said) by modern science of the burden of carrying malaria, they can devote all their time to making the most of you.

But even if you are not a mosquito, Arles has its gastronomic attractions. The most famous dish à l'Arlésienne, of course, was that girl in the Daudet play for which Bizet wrote the music. Otherwise it is a town where, in addition to the sort of food and drink you can enjoy anywhere else in Provence, there are one or two peculiar specialities. The most appetising of these is the saucisson d'Arles, one of the best of its kind in France (others come from Lyon, Strasbourg, Brittany, Lorraine), and there are garnishes which make the most of the local olive oil with aubergines and small whole tomatoes.

Summer 1965

Butter and Basil

However much one may be devoted to French food and wine, it is always good for the constitution to eat and drink in Italy from time to time.

We were just heading for a trattoria Toscana at Bordighera when we remembered that we were in Liguria and should obviously eat in a Genoese restaurant. This we did, and ate our pasta with that wonderful, peculiarly Genoese 'butter' (in the culinary sense) called pesto, which is made of oil, garlic, grated cheese, pine-seeds and – dominating all the other ingredients – the basil grown in Genoa, which is claimed to be richer and more subtly flavoured than basil grown anywhere else.

After luncheon, which also included good home-made salami, a veal cutlet, Taleggio cheese from Lombardy, and a bottle of Barolo from Piedmont that went well with everything, we turned westwards once more, stopping at a Ventimiglia ironmonger to buy a couple of those huge barrel-shaped aluminium cooking pots which are sold by weight in Italy and are big enough to stew a goose in.

Spring 1965

Paradise Regained?

Fontaine-de-Vaucluse is eighteen miles to the east of Avignon and takes its name from the spectacular spring which, my Baedeker of 1914 informs (and which I see no reason to doubt fifty years later), 'rising in a grand cirque of rocks 650 ft high, gushes forth from a cavern 25-30 ft wide.' The spring becomes a roaring full-blown river at once, full of trout, too cold and swift to encourage mosquitoes, and providing a wonderful setting for Mme Paradis' riverside hotel, the Hostellerie Le Château, and higher upstream *auprès des cascades*, M Philip's Restaurant des Jardins de Pétrarque (for in Fontaine, the poet first met Laura in 1327 and although she was married to the local Count, bearing him eleven children, he stayed on there to write love poems to her for twenty-one years!).

It was during an outstandingly good meal at Philip's that we first drank Gigondas, another admirable red Rhône wine from Vaucluse which, like Château-neuf-du-Pape, comes from vines apparently growing out of stones. These stones are deliberately put there for two purposes: to absorb heat during the day and so keep the ripening grape warm at night, and to prevent the evaporation of moisture from the red soil underneath them.

At the Hostellerie Le Château we drank the other good Vaucluse red wine, Cairanne, which was shown on the wine list as the 'sélection du patron'. We ate the 13-Franc menu – jambon cru des Alpilles (very local and delicious), trout meunière, and a dish announced on the menu as 'filet d'agneau' which turned out to be a simple côtelette d'agneau – a slip of the pen or technical lapse in the kitchen no doubt brought about by the excitement of Mme Paradis regained.

Autumn 1964

Hungry Work

Looking at theatres, like looking at churches or pictures, is exhausting work, and Mantua is as good a place to need refreshment and feel hungry in as any. They are great ones there for stuffing ravioli with unexpected things. Agnoli alla mantovana are filled with bacon, beef sauce, salamelle (which are delicious tiny salami), chickens' livers, cheese, egg yolk, and cooked in broth. A simpler filling, used for smaller ravioli called tortellini alla mantovana, is pumpkin, cheese, nutmeg and egg yolk. When it came to it we skipped the specialities and ate an enormous amount of very good full-size salami (none of your salamelle) with a litre and a half of local red wine that was entirely suited to our appetite and the food we appeased it with.

Autumn 1969

Even restaurants have legends which are kept alive, if not by the restaurants, at least by their customers. At St Jean-Cap-Ferrat, for instance, the restaurant known as Cappa's is famed for the variety of its hors-d'oeuvres, which you choose from a huge kind of mobile sideboard, answering 'yes' or 'no' as each item is offered to you.

The story goes that, to avoid interruption of the tête-à-tête he was enjoying with his pretty French guest, an English customer once told the waiter to give him a bit of everything on the hors-d'oeuvres trolley. The waiter did as he was asked. And the Englishman found himself faced with two large plates in front of him, piled high with generous helpings of each of the thirty or more different items of hors-d'oeuvres!

Cappa's has hardly changed at all in the thirty-six years I have known it. The bar, the kitchen, and the Messieurs and the Dames, are still across the street and the famous hors-d'oeuvres has lost none of its variety. When I first went there it was also renowned for its crêpes Suzette, a taste I have now rather grown out of, but which at the time was well worth indulging in. The pancake trolley offered almost every known liqueur from Abricotine to Zubrovka, and you were encouraged to have as many crêpes as you liked – with a different flavour every time.

Autumn 1970

Royal Sausages

I used to journey every Thursday from London to a little shed in a lane near the village of Much Hadham in Hertfordshire solely to buy a week's supply of a certain Mr Reed's sausages. Well, not quite *solely*; Thursday also happened to be market day five miles away at Bishop's Stortford (licensing hours 10.30 a.m. to 10.30 p.m.).

Looking back, and slightly over the top of rose-coloured glasses, I wonder whether those sausages were, in fact, flavoured with anything more unusual than sage. Probably not; yet they seem at this date to have been such stuff as Strasbourg patés are made on. But if English sausages don't taste like that, why on earth shouldn't they?

I have an English recipe dated 1830 for making pork sausages containing parsley, young onions, fine spices, truffles, and white wine – which was Hock, Moselle or Champagne, according to taste. And another for mutton sausages made with garlic, two anchovies, sweet herbs and a pint of oysters. And how about 'Royal Sausages' – made of (among other things) the meat of a partridge, a capon, gammon, leg of veal, parsley, chives, mushrooms, beaten spice and garlic? Add a few fennel seeds to any of these and you would have an English sausage to equal the finest finocchiona in Tuscany.

We must face it, however, that native charcuterie is not very imaginative in modern England. Indeed, the final and most shattering demonstration of the shopkeeper's joy in customer resistance is the continued, unabashed offer for sale of something called 'Bologna sausage' – as cynical and calculated an insult to the sausage-making capital of the world as can be imagined. (Mr Dolby, my 1830 cook, tells me that the final stage of his recipe for Bologna sausage is to rub the outside of the skins with a mixture of olive oil and the ashes of vine-twigs – a bit of a poet as well as a cook, obviously).

Autumn 1962

La Trompe

Vire, pop. 13,000 and 'twinned' with Totnes in Devon, was nine-tenths destroyed ('sinistré' is the expressive French word) during the war. Among the places rebuilt was the Hotel *Cheval Blanc* (recommended in the 1896 Baedeker), but, it seemed to us, on something of a shoe-string. Our bathroom had no proper door, only a pair of those knee-length swinging saloon-door affairs you see in Westerns, fixed on such powerful springs that they crashed shut with a noise like a gun-shot unless you were careful. The din was nothing, however, compared with the machine-gun rattle of air-locks whenever anybody in the hotel turned on a tap.

I have finally reached the conclusion that the French just have no talent for plumbing. No nation, I have now decided, uses a greater variety of lavatory cisterns with less effect; offers more high level models that never fill; more low-level models that never stop filling with the noise of a jet-plane taking off; more cylinders fixed to the wall which blare like a brass-band when flushed (a popular type is proudly and appropriately named by its maker 'La Trompe').

Spring/Summer 1974

A Toast!

Old Compton's Fancy, October

Above all, October is the period of the vintage, and what begins a year better than that?

So it happens that every October, as the wine, Old Compton and his wife celebrate becoming a year older, the cellar gets a couple of irreplaceable bottles smaller, and toasts are drunk to the immortal memory of a father-in-law who thoughtfully bequeathed several *precieuses bouteilles* of claret to be drunk on such occasions.

It was a bequest, what is more, with an unexpected bonus. Not only was there wine in the cellar; it was also discovered put away in the drawers, first of one odd bit of furniture, then of another, in unused rooms all over the house where the temperature was right. A magnum of Haut-Brion 1947 found in the bottom of a wardrobe now lies patiently in a bin under the stairs at Old Compton's.

Autumn 1972

Toastmaster

Edgar Allan Tennyson

Toastmaster! What are you roaring now, in a voice like the trump of doom?

'The gent who spat in Sir George's hat will kindly leave the room!';
But neither the angels in heaven above, nor the demons down under

217

the sea,
Can ever dissever my soul from the soul of the beautiful Annabel
Lee.

An Excuse for the Glass

in anticipation of a plethora of summit meetings during 1958

Ian R. Hamilton

He is a small man, pink faced with blue eyes beaming bonhomie.
While ladling out robust quips to the surging mob around him, he
raises his glass to 'Peace and International Friendship.' This is, of
course, a caricature of M Nikita Khrushchev, insisting on drinking yet
another toast in undiluted vodka and ostentatiously draining his glass
every time *do dna* – to the bottom.

These B. and K. diplomatic parties, with their prolific toasting, in
the Kremlin's St Geogre's Hall are now a recognised part of the Soviet
political scene; practised students of Moscow life insist they have to be
seen to be believed.

In England the toast has become rather more of a formality. None
who has heard it can forget the sonorous voice of the toastmaster at the
Mansion House, or the double toast at the Annual Pilgrim's Dinner,
'The Queen and The President'.

There are the informal toasts in restaurant, bar, or pub, the
'Cheers',, the 'Bung Ho', the 'Down the Hatch', the 'Here's Luck';
they appear frequently pointless, but are none the less sincere even if
they sound mediocre compared with the more sublime toasts of the
past ...

> Here's to the maiden of bashful fifteen,
> > Here's to the widow of fifty,
> Here's to the flaunting extravagant queen,
> > Here's to the housewife that's thrifty.
>
> > Let the toast pass,
> > > Drink to the lass,
> > I warrant she'll prove
> > > An excuse for the glass.

218

But where did the pleasant habit of toasting and health drinking, which lends a certain charm to an often mundane occasion, have its beginning?

The next time you are called upon to drink a toast at a dinner or banquet you might give a thought to the ancient Greeks and Romans among whom this pleasant custom had its origin.

In their decline, the luxury loving Romans at their *commissationes* really went to town and seem to have had little difficulty in finding an excuse for the cup; they toasted their gods, their friends and the beauties of the day in endless session. A favourite feature of these bouts was to drink a pledge in wine for every letter in the name of the one being toasted.

If health drinking in England had its origin in Roman customs, Saxon drinking practices certainly had some influence as well. There's the hoary old story of that period of how Rowena, the accomplished and beautiful daughter of the Saxon leader Hengist, offered to drink a toast to the British king, Vortigern, at a banquet given in his honour by her father. The king, intoxicated by the variety of drinks and Rowena's beauty agreed to the toast. He himself then took the cup from her, kissed her and drank from it freely. So enamoured was Vortigern with the lady that he asked for her hand in marriage. This was as the Saxon had planned, and in return for his consent he received the province of Kent.

Not so happy is the one about the murder of a young King Edward in AD 978, engineered by his stepmother, Elfrida, so that her own son might wear the crown of England. She made a great show of hospitality during a visit Edward made to her at Corfe Castle on a hunting expedition. Then, while drinking a farewell cup of wine from the saddle, the king was stabbed in the back.

In fact, at one time, the drinking of healths was regarded more as a convenience for getting rid of unwanted associates. To guard against treachery it became the custom for a person drinking a toast to ask two of his friends to pledge his safety. Normally, three people would rise when a health was drunk; the pledger faced the drinker, while a friend stood on guard at his back. A further precaution was that surrounding the ceremony of the loving cup. In this case each guest rose and bowed to the immediate neighbour on his right; each, in turn, removed the cover with his right hand while the other drank. He who drank a toast was glad to have the assurance that the right or dagger hand of his neighbour was occupied in holding the lid of the chalice. These two customs are still observed by the City Livery Companies at their banquets.

In the early seventeenth century health drinking became an even more ceremonious affair in England. Often toasts would be drunk solemnly on bended knee. And in Scotland, there was, and is, a custom of toasting with one foot on the table and one on the chair – a precaution, no doubt, against excessive repetition.

As would be expected during the Protectorate, England became a pretty sober country. But the Restoration revived public drinking and with it the drinking of loyal toasts.

The application of the word 'toast' to health drinking dates back to the reign of Charles II, and was at first a reference to the custom of drinking to the ladies. An account of what happened at Bath is given by Steele in *The Tatler* of 1709.

> It happened, that on a Publick Day a celebrated Beauty of those times was in the Cross-Bath, and one of the Crowd of her Admirers took a Glass of the Water in which the Fair One stood, and drank her Health to the Company. There was in the Place a Gay Fellow, half fuddled, who offered to jump in, and swore, Tho' he liked not the Liquor, he would have the Toast (meaning the lady herself). He was opposed in his Resolution; yet this whim gave Foundation to the present Honour which is done to the Lady we mention in our Liquors, who has ever since been called a 'Toast'.

At a later date, it became a University custom to put toast in loving-cups, and in tankards of beer to improve, so it was thought, the flavour of the contents.

The stories of secret drinkings of health to the exiled Stuarts during the Hanoverian period are legion. One is of George II, at a public masquerade, taking a lady aside for a glass of wine. Not knowing the identity of her courteous partner she invited him to toast the Old Pretender. 'With all my heart,' the King replied, 'I am always happy to drink to the health of unfortunate princes.'

At the turn of the nineteenth century the custom of drinking healths and proposing toasts, especially in Scottish society, was tyrannically enforced. To take a glass of wine during dinner without previously dedicating it to the health of someone at the table was regarded as a breach of etiquette.

A catalogue of actual Toasts, the customs, traditions and variations in their drinking, has yet to be compiled – certainly not here. Meanwhile, gentlemen, a toast! *To Sweethearts and Wives, and may they never meet!*

Spring 1958

Coffee
and
Liqueurs

Old Compton's Fancy, March

This is the month when Old Compton's accelerator foot begins to itch. He dreams not so much of Paris, where the problem of parking almost outweighs for him the manifold delights, as of the long straight roads that lead through Burgundy, Savoy and the Alps down to the pleasures of Lombardy and Venetia.

He feels that sudden longing for lemon trees and those delicious white dried figs of Italy, the dark-eyed beauties who flood the Piazza San Marco in the spring dusk, and the singing voices of the workmen as they cycle home without lights in terrifying phalanxes that spread right across the road.

Old Compton once had a friend who turned his impulses into a fine art. One night this friend was forced to attend a boring party in Paris. He was wafted on to a highly fashionable but equally boring night-club. By about one o'clock in the morning, X could stand no longer the thumping drums and the vinegary chatter. He slipped out of the place, hailed a cab and commanded: 'To Italy!'

Obediently the cabman drove X to the Porte d'Italie. He was about to put down his flag and put out his hand, when X said: 'Continue my friend! We're on our way to Venice!'

The driver, who possessed a keen sense of the conventions, seemed put out. 'Not in a tail coat and white tie, you can't,' he said. 'Besides, you have no luggage.' 'Don't you want to see Venice?' X asked, flourishing notes in front of him.

With a perfunctory grumble, the taxi-man settled back into his seat, muttering that all the English were mad, and away they trundled down Route Nationale No 7.

They stopped for sublime meals – it was in the days before the French had taken to instant coffee and hot dogs. X's shirt and white waistcoat slowly turned yellow in the dust; his white tie drooped. But finally they reached a Palladian villa on the Brenta where in circumstances of almost farm-like simplicity, the Paris taximan had the time of his life.

Consolations Chez Lui

Alas! Such fantasies are beyond the stretch of today's travel allowance. But if Venice or Rome are beyond him for the moment, O.C. will console himself by a meal that at least will evoke for him the roads of France in the spring....

He will peel, wash in acidulated water and gently boil 2 lbs of so-called winter artichokes. For five minutes he will boil eight fresh eggs; he will plunge them into cold water to remove their shells. He will lay eggs and artichokes in a pan together, season, mask with a thick Mornay sauce, and put under the grill until the sauce begins to brown and to bubble. A Batard-Montrachet 1959 would gracefully accompany this dish.

Next, he would obtain from one of the French butchers in Soho a real pre-sale – none of your overfat English joints, so corrupted by farmers' subsidies that lamb has become virtually indistinguishable from mutton. He would slip unpeeled garlic under the beauty, and sprinkle it with rosemary. If properly roasted, so that a hint of pink lingers about the flesh like the last memory of a sunset, no sauce, beyond the gravy, should be necessary. Here he would experiment with one of the 1964 clarets. There would also be a salad of Belgian endives and walnuts, in a plain French dressing.

Lastly, a cheese platter, with Brie and Petits Suisses – all of which come to perfection around the equinox, and can be found finer in England than in France.

Spring 1967

Meals to Remember

Nancy Spain

who discloses the prandial frustrations of a woman journalist

Related to both Samuel ('Self Help') Smiles and Mrs ('Cookbook') Beeton. Roedean indicted her 'speaks before she thinks' and Noel Coward as 'outrageously flippant'. Qualities which, after two best-sellers, *Thank You Nelson* and *Mrs Beeton and Her Husband*, and eight detective stories, made her Beaverbrook's *enfant terrible* of Fleet Street with a penchant for debunking the self-important. Loved celebrities, cricket, lacrosse, travel and – unavailingly – Gilbert Harding; rejected $47,000 US syndicate offer for Princess Margaret–Peter Townsend story; broadcast regularly; appeared in Bertram Mills' Circus and Sinbad on Ice. Loved life!

I have noticed that when people are asked to contribute to a series with a title like 'Meals to Remember' they start sucking their teeth. Does some tiny fragment of cold boiled lobster linger in a hollow tooth to remind them of the Eton and Harrow Match when Roger made seventy-seven and carried his bat, or the time we all packed (screaming with laughter) into that Greek boy's Lagonda and drove madly into Berkshire to call on Compton Mackenzie? Not on your Nelly. First, people brush their teeth more often than that. Second, the happy meals are *not* the ones we remember.

Oh no. The meals on my mind are those which were disastrous. Apart from anything else, good journalists seldom eat. Slightly soiled in our beige mackintoshes we have long ago learnt the knack of existing on a double Scotch for nine hours. We are hardened to packets of potato chips, battered purple-wrapped milk chocolate with nuts in, and little furtive bags of mixed raisins and almonds.

Why, one of the meals I best remember is a lamb chop eaten (and most daintily, too) by Miss Vivien Leigh in her dressing room when she was making *Anna Karenina*. I had been driven there in the studio car. The paper had told me to go and congratulate her on becoming a Ladyship. There was some mess-up. I had no lunch. After I had kicked my heels for five hours, Miss Leigh received me at 3.30 p.m. In front of me she ate a lamb chop, new potatoes, peas and she drank a glass of some white wine. She then ate peaches and said she could not have cream because of the corsets she was wearing as the unhappy and

225

suicidal Anna. Seldom has any hungry journalist been nearer suicide than me....

* * *

The social indiscretion of all time actually happened at Wheeler's. I was sitting on the second floor (believe it or not) sipping Chablis and eating superb Sole Gondu when I heard three people discussing me in no uncertain terms. 'Oh,' said one, who turned out to be the features editor of a fashion magazine, 'she's terribly pathetic really, always getting thrown out of nightclubs in those jeans. And then, of course, her excuse is that they're clean, my dear.'

'I think she sounds quite sensible on the wireless,' said another, who turned out to be the author of a book called *Strange Evil*. 'And whatever you may say about her,' said the third, who was a representative of my own publishers, 'She's really terribly, terribly nice to children.'

After such a splendid recommendation, there was really nothing else I could do except rise to my feet and join them for the rest of lunch. We all ate strawberries and cream.

Autumn 1957

Meals to Remember

Alec Waugh

Shortly after leaving Sherborne, created a furore with *Loom of Youth* which was constantly in print until 1962 – but earned him only £1000. Despite that, still more famous brother Evelyn wrote, 'I have never shared his tastes in friends or in women. But in the years of my poverty and obscurity I was constantly at his table.'

Travelled widely, and found further success with *Island in the Sun* (a runaway best-seller) and an autobiography, *The Best Wine Last*.

Of many such occasions I remember in particular a lunch in Marseilles in the early spring of 1930. I was catching a French steamer for Mombasa. It was to sail at four o'clock. I had travelled down by the night train from Paris. I was to be out of Europe for ten weeks. Previous experience of French ships and British colonies warned me that during that period my celibacy was unlikely to be relieved; an anticipation that was incidentally fulfilled. I planned for myself an appropriate farewell – a bouillabaisse on Basso's balcony on the Vieux Port, then a sampling of the varied pleasures that were offered in the network of narrow streets on the right side of the harbour for which the contemporary traveller will search in vain. I had not however taken into account the excellence of Basso's bouillabaisse.

Bouillabaisse is my favourite lunch dish. I have eaten it in many places, but not even in Garrac's in Nice have I tasted one that was more succulent and pungent. It was made without langouste. Langouste increases the cost considerably and in my opinion does not improve the taste. The langouste loses its own delicate flavour, but its flesh is too firm to absorb the soup in the way that that of the softer *rascase* does. I ordered a local white wine – Bellet. The bite of the saffron made me thirsty; I ordered a second half-litre. I lingered over it, savouring each mouthful while my thoughts moved in easy freedom from one subject to another. Five minutes to two. If I was to visit the Vieux Port, I should have to hurry. I hesitated, but only for a moment; so excellent a meal could not be hurried. It had to be given its proper climax. I called for a cognac; and as I sipped it, I looked without envy at the cluster of narrow streets beyond the masts.

* * *

One of my best friends was H.S. Mackintosh, a fellow Sherbournian, known then as an athlete, a man of charm, and someone 'employed profitably in the city'. He was anxious to persuade a young person of considerable attractions that she would be wise to link her fate with his.

He therefore arranged an elaborate dinner at the Carlton. His guests included athletes and 'men in business'; and, since she had contributed short stories to the *Sketch*, he was anxious that a writer should adjust the balance. I was therefore an essential cog in his campaign. I greatly looked forward to the occasion. But unaccountably and almost undeservedly I was smitten that afternoon with a violent attack of nausea. At six o'clock I was fit for one thing only – to curl up in a solitary bed and sleep; but loyalty demanded my presence at the Carlton. I laced myself into a white waistcoat and went out to battle.

There were ten other guests. It was a five-course dinner. It started with consommé Henri quartre. As I gazed into its limpid pool, I fancied that never had so many contributing flavours been more harmoniously blended. If only I could taste it! A poached sole was garnished with shrimps and grapes. A duck was accompanied by an orange salad. How firm yet how tender its flesh looked. It was the English fashion then to serve a sweet before a savoury. The cocktail party with its attendant canapés was not yet known. The sweet was a soufflé surprise. It was hot and steaming on the surface; inside a core of ice. The savouries since it was autumn were grilled mushrooms, sprinkled with red pepper.

A different wine was served with every course. Sherry with the soup, Meursault with the sole, Burgundy with the duck, a Château Rayne-Vigneau with the soufflé, Champagne with the savoury. At the very end I sipped a glass of Champagne. It was all I dared. 'Was the dinner as supreme as it appeared?' I asked myself, as dish after dish passed untouched before my weakened eyes. I was then very much under the influence of George Moore. Had not the Master said that the woman who laid the greatest hold on one was she who had denied one? If my palate had been unimpaired, my appetite unchecked, might I not have found some failing, some slight imperfection in the sole or savoury? Can perfection exist on this imperfect planet? I shall never know. But that unsavoured meal will remain in my memory for ever, to be recalled most fondly, to be regretted most.

Autumn 1960

Donovan's

C. Gordon Glover

And this is the way of it at Donovan's, a strange and not unfriendly war of attrition between guests and management; and if you want your breakfast on Sunday before 10.30 and decide to cook it yourself, you'll find that Mareen has locked the kitchen door and taken the key with her and the rest of the family to Mass. And if you don't want your 'tea' at six, then tea at six you will have unless you win the daily skirmish for bacon-and-eggs at seven-thirty. Each day is an adventure at Donovan's as the sea booms against the splendour of the off-shore islands, and the morning chickens peck about the unswept debris of last night's bar, and the grey donkeys wander the lanes between their hedges of heavy fuchsia flowers and bank-sides thick with the red and yellow flares of wild montbretia. And there are the heads of seals bobbing in the clear green water of the tiny harbour where the upturned curraghs are lashed, up-ended, to the jetty and lie there like dead dolphins with the spines of their keels shining in the windy summer sun.

You will see and hear many strange things, like cock-crow in the morning, and the banshee wailing of curlews in the hills which could be the voices of the ghosts of the pre-history people who lived about this wilderness.

The Full Treatment

Donovan's is no place for the pampered sybarite or the gastronome. But it casts its dotty spell over all who may at first be shocked by, and then come to love, the wildly improbable. Like returning for bacon and eggs at seven-thirty to find the whole establishment bolted and barred with the whole family out and caught up with Murphy in the town. There's nothing to be done then but drive the three miles to the next pub in the next village and tell your forlorn tale to the proprietor, beg a pie of him, and hear him say: 'So it's locked out of Donovan's that you are, is it? Well, well, but he's the cool man right enough, that Sheamus Donovan.'

Somehow you bear it all with fortitude, even with relish, for this is living. And living, indeed, it is as the shadows of evening fall over Donovan's, and gradually the great gaunt bar begins to fill up. First with the old men of the sea, the men of the curraghs, who walk in one by one to lift pints of dark draught stout in their knotty paws, and then to sit, side by side and bolt upright on hard-backed chairs, their faces lined and lean as the heads of hawks, their old eyes blue and red-rimmed with the scouring of the spindrift and the brine. They sit still as statues with an air of ancient remoteness and nobility, and when they talk to one another it is in the Irish tongue, for they know no other, and soft and strange is the sound of it.

There are hoof-beats from donkeys and ponies bearing people in little carts to an evening at Donovan's. From miles around they come in from the hills, more of them and more of them, the girls in head-scarves and the young men in thick jerseys and jeans, and the fathers and mothers of them, too, come in to Donovan's from heaven knows where. Mickeen and Mareen pull the pints, and pour the smokey whiskey into the rough glasses, and soon there's not a seat in the place which hums now like a hive of huge bees.

Wild Music

Very soon the music will start – a young man with a squeeze-box, another with a tin whistle, an older man with a fiddle. The ceiling is low and the cacophony between it and the closed doors and windows ear-splitting. You are strangely happy, though, to sit beaten into helpless submission by the din, glass in hand, eyes smarting with smoke as they watch the exuberance of all about them. You hear forlorn and ancient airs, and songs of seals, and then the assault of a faster, merrier, blood-tingling tempo as the music for the reels opens up from the farthest corner, and the young men and their bog-myrtle girls are on their feet with the quick-step, kick-step Kerry dances. Laughter sounds red as cock-crow as the Brigids, Maeves and Mareens step it up with the Michaels, Patricks and Shauns from the next village and from the chubby little farm houses standing in their patches of potatoes and windy oats.

It is said about these parts: 'What's the hurry? Divil, and the man who made time made plenty of it.' Yet, surprisingly, and at the hour of 11.30 precisely it *is* 'Time' at Donovan's. The music stops, the glasses are drained, the head-scarves are adjusted, and the company ebbs away in a steady river, to vanish down the fuchsia-bordered lanes to heaven knows where.

Only the old men of the sea, still as statues, sit it out until the very end, drawing at their short pipes and last long porters. With their sea-blue, red-rimmed eyes they sit there in Donovan's, archetypes of a way of life little changing in the thunder of the breakers and the spume of brine against the cliffs of this 'last outpost in Europe and next parish to America'.

Summer 1968

Maxim's Comes to Town

Pat Davis

Maxim's, the epitome of all luxury restaurants! Opened in Paris in 1893 by a young waiter, Maxine, who shrewdly anglicised his name, (and more recently swept onwards by France's world-famous couturier Pierre Cardin) it was a magnet for Parisian society and the internationally chic.

Here, to see and to be seen, came princes and politicians, financiers and film stars. And, of course, elegant women – dressed by Poiret. It was an era of ostrich feathers and white greyhounds, of mountains of hat-boxes and rich Russian leather trunks. Of pilgrimages from Cannes and Chamonix, from the gaming tables of Monte Carlo and the spas of Germany to the shrine of luxury and opulence that was Maxim's, before journeying to Longchamp and Ascot.

It was the forerunner of Art Nouveau's comet course. A ferment of ideas, of invention and verve, of utilisation of new materials. A revolt against the dead hand of academic art and naturalism: a crusade to create a world of universal happiness and beauty, to capture the quintessence of Nature in its slender, interlacing lines.

From such a melting pot of ideas, architect Louis Marnez created his dream restaurant. With suffused lighting from golden fleurs de lys and huge circular wall mirrors, rich red velvet banquettes and dark veneered wood, it held a feeling of warm privacy even within its ensemble. On the walls, Louis Sonnier's bleached landscapes were peopled with delicately nude girls less obviously sensuous for all their nudity than the fashionable ladies below them with their pulled in wasp-waists and mature bosoms thrust forward to exaggerate every female curve. Maxim's breathed an atmosphere of intimacy; hinted a touch of naughtiness.

Over it presided Albert and Roger, high priests and despots, who with the flicker of a trained eye could sum up status and pretension – and with a wave of the hand consign lesser lights to the social oblivion of distant tables. Waiters, deft and dextrous as magicians, performed their ritual with such silent discipline as to be invisible. And behind the scenes there were chefs, such chefs, eager to serve patrons gifted with the true understanding and appreciation of this zenith of French classical cuisine. And it may well have been at Maxim's that Nubar Gulbenkian quipped: 'The best number for a dinner party is two – myself and a damn good waiter'.

The luxurious dining-room with its *fin de siècle* décor welcomed royalty and *nouveau riche*, stars and socialites alike, ranging from Edward VII to the Duke and Duchess of Windsor, from Marlene Dietrich to Nureyev, from Lady Docker to Jackie Onassis. It welcomed too a young man who celebrated his majority by having served to him, on a silver platter, a young damsel *au naturel* (and, in those pre-bikini days, presumably very 'rare' indeed). And another who signalled the end of the glories of his bachelordom by drinking champagne in a coffin.

In the Faubourg Saint-Honoré, there was also Maxim's shop which had once been the Charpentier Art Gallery. Unkind tongues suggested that the cost of the latter's fine paintings never rivalled those of Maxim's exorbitantly expensive sardines – the best in the world. If there was a hint of the plebeian in sardines there was none in Maxim's freshly fragrant Russian caviar, Norwegian salmon, duck foie gras, exotic fruits, bitter mocha wafers, sherry vinegar, or – milk's leap to immortality – rare cheeses.

Today, Maxim's the legend has come to London (as it already has to Peking and will to Moscow). Panton Street, between the Haymarket and Leicester Square, holds just the right hint of refinement preparing for a header into the whirlpool of night life. Art Nouveau flourishes anew in the elegantly recreated restaurant which seats 200. Even a palm-court orchestra, a mirror to the times, unobtrusively soothes ear and heart to echo the true Maxim's atmosphere. Above lie a champagne bar and private dining suites. The wine list is as long as it is discerning.

Nor is it surprising that Christian Paul Moury, one of a family of seven chefs, a Vice-President of the Academie Culinaire de France, with experience ranging from the Trianon Palace at Versailles to London's Savoy and Carlton Towers, should, as Chef de Cuisine, have introduced his own light and imaginative creations. To him, cooking is still an act of love; one that must be entered into with abandon or not at all.

Restaurant managers Hervé Salez and Jean François Pierry uphold Maxim's finest traditions and add a soupçon of discreet modernity. Hervé was recently General Manager at the Legends Club. There he achieved a double meed of fame. Initially, for his cocktail recipes. Later, for his smooth handling of Elizabeth Taylor's exuberant fiftieth birthday party.

Jean François was gifted with a flying start by first seeing light of day in Lyons, gastronomic capital of France. National Service interrupted his early apprenticeship but even this he turned to good use as private Head Waiter to General de Boisfleury now a power in the Ministry of Defence. In this country, he has seen more peaceful service at Hintlesham Hall, Ipswich, and Eastwell Manor, Ashford, in Kent.

Maxim's was launched into the fullness of the London season with the party of the year. A guest list which included Princess Fizyal of Jordan, Prince Adyn Aga Khan, the Duke and Duchess of Marlborough, Edouard de Rothschild, Lord and Lady Spencer Churchill, Princess Ira von Furstenberg, Countess Jioconda Cigogne, Faye Dunaway, Charlotte Rampling ... made it look as if *Debrett*, *Almanak de Gotha*, *Who's Who In The Theatre* and the *Annuaire de la Noblesse* had had a joyous get together. Not surprising perhaps that the cloakroom had been prudently insured for a quiet million!

And though many guests stepped out of their Rolls-Royces, Pierre Cardin was content to opt for delivery by a refurbished Maxim's 1920 van. And piquant was his meeting with his English counterpart, Hardy Amies. Thereafter 200 guests sat down, as *The Times* neatly put it, to 'a nap-hand of traditional haute cuisine'.

To come down to less star-spangled levels let it be noted that Maxim's make no pretensions to cuisine copyright. Some of their secrets will doubtless be revealed to students who join their Chelsea School of Cookery. Nor are those delights confined to Panton Street. Their outside catering department added an extra touch of glamour to the marqueed banks of the Thames at Henley where, moored midstream, the London Sinfonia Orchestra doubtless played Handel's 'Water Music'.

Today, a visit to this fabled restaurant is as memorable a gastronomic and social occasion as it was in Paris in its heyday.

'Supper at Maxim's' is still the lure few women can refuse.

Summer 1983

Stateside Eating

Max Hastings

Every American asks a visitor how he likes the food. I just say what every European must have been saying for years: 'The steaks are great!' Having dodged the issue that way, one is at a slight loss for a follow-up. I've eaten at a fairly wide cross-section of American restaurants, some modest, all expensive, and I feel it's only charitable to suggest that Communist agents have infiltrated even American kitchens. If I were asked to go further than that, I would just ask when a restaurant in Minneapolis which charges £6 for an unambitious dinner for two is going to learn to add an 's' to 'Beaujolai' on its wine list.

I was lucky enough to be born at a time when cheap wine was starting to come into England in quantity. Thus to dine in America is torture. Even when being lavishly entertained in the most affluent household, you may be invited to drown yourself in pre-prandial Dry Martini, but you will eat on iced water and like it.

To ask for a wine list at an American restaurant seems to be to demand cabaret rather than a drink. At one otherwise very good eating-place, St Emilion was considered a little difficult for the clientele to pronounce, so Sant-ay-meel-lee-on was printed underneath. And there is seldom any way of knowing whether you are to enjoy an 1867 or a 1967 Burgundy. Americans seem to find the strain of distinguishing between Californian and French champagne quite enough of a battle for one evening.

Still, one is at least never short on coffee. If you can prevent the waiter from bringing coffee with the shrimp cocktail, it's a victory. If you can restrain him until after the steak, it's a triumph.

But, as always, it was Art Buchwald who chronicled the American culinary disaster in his account of the President interviewing a candidate for White House chef. The cook was listing his skill with quenelles de brochet, noisettes d'agneau, and soufflé Grand Marnier, when Johnson interrupted: 'Yes, we know all that, but how do you feel about okra with black-eyed peas?'

'I am sorry, but I never concern myself with politics ...'

My own problem, too, is that I just don't happen to like okra with black-eyed peas.

Summer 1967

Life begins at 21

Headmaster: Hastings, you are neither black not white. Merely grey.

Housemaster: I will not say of him as was said of Kipling that all the good fairies came to his christening and they were all drunk. Just that many came and none were quite sober.

Editor: Many books (including *Bomber Command* which won the Somerset Maugham Prize, and *Overlord* and *Falkland Islands* which both became the *Yorkshire Post*'s Book of the Year) and many worldwide journalistic forays later, the grey sheep became Editor of the *Daily Telegraph*!

The British Epicure Society

Merlin Minshall

1 May

In 1957 Mr Aslan, an architect and member of the Society, purchased a
house just off Piccadilly Circus. Built in the reign of Charles II this
house had become a ruin. Mr Aslan restored it to its original state and
added an Italianate roof garden.

'Would it not be a gesture,' I said to him one day, 'for the Society to
organise an official re-opening ceremony?'

'Why not?'

And on May Day the Mayor of Westminster himself came in full
regalia (with his beautiful wife) and in the presence of the President of
the Society, Sir Albert Richardson, performed the re-opening
ceremony.

Afterwards we went next door for a Restoration Dinner at the
Comedy Restaurant. We started off with a traditional Turtle Soup
that would have been the envy of Dick Whittington himself. This was
followed by Sole Inigo Jones and then by Surrey Chicken Breasts done
after a recipe favoured by Christopher Wren.

7 May 1962

Anyone who has read his Pepys diary knows that Pepys was by way of
being a bit of an epicure. I thought therefore that it would be well in
the traditions of the Club to hold a 'Pepysian Dinner' in which every
item was contemporary.

I found that on 10 March 1664, Pepys wrote: 'Home to dinner with
my wife, to a good Hog's Harslet.' I further discovered that this
consisted of the heart, liver and brains fried in a light batter. 'A piece
of meat that I love,' Pepys described it.

Then on 10 March 1660, he wrote: 'So I went to a special good dinner with a Mr Veezy, a leg of veal and bacon, capons, sausages and fritters, with abundance of wine.'

On 1 May 1669, Pepys served as part of a 'pretty merry evening,' a Syllabub. 'Cost me 12s.,' he wrote.

Finally one reads that on 7 July 1665, Pepys took notice 'to what a condition it hath pleased God to bring me at this time!' And how does he assess this? Why by noting down the contents of his cellar, which contained he tells us: 'two tierces of Claret, two quarter casks of Canary, and a smaller vessel of Sack; a vessel of Tent and another of Malaga.'

And so on 7 May 300 years later twenty members of the British Epicure Society sat down at the **Cocke Tavern** in Fleet Street, which was well known to Pepys, and had a dinner that as near as possible reproduced these extracts. Entirely unrehearsed was one of our members noticing that opposite to her was hung the portrait of a most elegant Young gentleman. It was none other than the Mr Veezy with whom Pepys had dined on 6 March 1660.

It's a small world, and if we had more dinners such as this (one cannot help feeling) there would be less dyspepsia.

Autumn 1962

Angel on the Rack

Nancy Andrew

An Angel took a job washing up in a small, very select restaurant. She folded her wings, put on a plastic apron and straightway the race was on.

Oh, sighed the Angel. Fish gear, fish gear, service spoons, service spoons. No service spoons to be seen anywhere at all. Coffee cups, coffee cups. Found one in the sink-o. Lipstick. Knock it off. One for the pig bin.

Cigars for the dry bin. (One for the wet bin), paté for the pigs, and one for the road. Corks for the pigs and caviar the dry bin, Château de la Maltroye, some left for the pigs.

Plate rack, on the rack, in the rack and out the rack. No, my lord waiter, I haven't any spoons. Knives go in this one, found one dessert spoon. Where go the toothpicks? Irrecoverably lost.

Hard rolls, soft rolls, french rolls, rock and rolls. Baa-baa black sheep, have you any teeth?

Boom go the large plates, bang go the small plates. Crash go cigar bands. Cymbals for the pigs.

Lobster shells, fish tails, young wives' tails and old wives' tails. Banana skins and olive stones and grapes all tête-à-tête. Orange peel and apple core and fruit salad encore. (This little piggy went to market for a date.)

Pooh, sighed the Angel (treading on a lost sole), camembert's no incense, and there's butter on my wings.

Round the bend, in the bin, up the stairs, down the stairs. Up the wall, down the hatch.

Help! said the Angel and she unfolded her wings, threw her plastic apron in the pig bin and flew back to heaven.

Summer 1961

Cigars

Old Compton's Fancy, February

Like his 'The British Epicure Society' feature in this magazine, Mr Minshall's *The Complete Book of Pasta* is full of fascinating stories and facts you never knew before. Not just about Cicero's fondness for *laganum*, the *tagliatelle* of his day, but, for instance, about when Pope Clement VII went to Paris to visit his niece Catherine de Medici and gave a great formal dinner for her and her husband, the Dauphin:

> At some point in the interminable menu, two dishes of pasta were served. One of them was dressed, exactly as it might be today, with the juice from the roast meat and grated cheese. The other was dressed with butter, sugar, honey, saffron and cinnamon.

Then there is Tasso's charming account of how tortellini came to be invented.

> Venus was still wandering, a disconsolate and forgotten exile, in the world of the Middle Ages. An inn-keeper, inflamed by her beauty, stole upstairs to gaze on her through the keyhole of her bedroom door. Venus was indeed there in all her glorious nudity. But the poor innkeeper's field of vision through the keyhole was so restricted that all he could see – was her navel!

Even that, though, was enough to inspire him; he retired to his kitchen to create tortellini which reproduce, to this day, that splendid navel.

Spring 1974

Side-lights on Cigars

Walter Kahn

Ladies scantily dressed, ladies of virtue – supposedly its own reward but here surrounded by a display of medals – dear old gentlemen with droopy moustaches, South American revolutionaries, characters from Shakespeare – unlikely bed fellows, you would think, except perhaps on Sunday television. But, in fact, these good people have, by tradition, for long adorned the bedizened labels of countless cigar boxes. How their quaint designs and curious subjects originated is a facet of the cigar trade lost in limbo.

You would think that cigar boxes are purely functional; designed to protect cigars, something to keep them in. But the cigar boxes that you and I cherish are covered with a wealth of exotic labels designed, presumably, to distract us from the main business of opening the box and coming to grips with the cigar. These labels are so cunningly fixed that it is virtually impossible to open the box without infinite patience, sharp knives, a device to tell where the lid is and an ample supply of loose cigars to keep us going while trying to open the box. (The afficionado amongst cigar smokers usually buys his cigars in plain square boxes of fifty, neatly tied with a silk ribbon. This box is called a *correderas* and is rather kinder to the cigars as it allows them to condition and mature much more evenly.)

Finally, a word on the subject of size names. In England more nonsense is talked about cigars and fewer smoked than anywhere else in the world. A Corona to the free cigar world is a shape. To us it is a size. Foreigners regard a Corona as a straight-shaped cigar of varying length. We know that it is really a five and a half inch long cigar. With us it follows that a Half Corona should obviously be two and three-quarter inches long. It is not. It is three and a half inches. A Petit Corona is five inches and a Double Corona varies from six and a half inches to a giant ten inches. It's not fair. Not content with these misleading names, up pop the importers with yet more names like Emeralds, Fabulosos, Mundiales, Gigantes, Curisidades Chicas, and many others.

As more and more women take to smoking cigars, it seems presumptuous to tender advice on selecting cigars as gifts for their menfolk. But when they are in doubt I would suggest they employ a touch of guile. For instance, if they want love and affection why not give Romeo y Julieta? If their man is timid what about Bolivar or Monte Cristo? To instil a more light-hearted approach to life why not Punch; and for Americans, Henry Clay every time? But for safety, give them La Corona, for there you have name, size and shape all rolled into one.

Summer 1959

Envoi

The Guv'nor!

Pat Davis

A *Wheeler's Review* anthology can end only in one way – with a six-foot, blue-eyed giant, Bernard Walsh. A man who liked his fellow men – and who in turn was respected and loved by them. A man who wholeheartedly seized opportunity and life – and in his enjoyment of them gave others much pleasure.

But he was born with no silver spoon in his mouth. In fact, his grandfather was an Irish horse-cooper famed for his high-stepping carriage pairs whose cunningly matching colours were undoubtedly aided on occasion by judicious application of dyes. His father, who disapproved of relations, because 'they always want something' traded in oysters close to the mud and shingle 'clike' shore of that home of oysters, Whitstable. Why was his shop called Wheeler's and not Walsh? Mystery surrounds the original Victorian Wheeler whose name is still over the Whitstable premises. He certainly owned an oyster boat; he may have killed himself by falling over his own gun!

As a boy, Bernard passed long days on the beach packing scores of oysters into oak barrels, baiting 200 hooks, or digging a couple of thousand lug worms between tides. School he let wash over him like the sea in which he swam and rowed with the best. But his lifelong affair with the oyster was still only calf-love.

For first, of all things, this 'young scallywag of the tidelines' who delighted in the challenge of the sea, coursed whippets, and hit monstrous drives on the Seasalter 'nine-holer' became a 'hoofer', a chorus boy. One, however, who soon turned a shrewd brain to stage management and a good voice to small speaking parts.

Despite the glamour of the stage, the still small voice of the oyster became steadily more insistent. And still more insistent was the voice of a pretty chorus girl (Ena) in the *Desert Song* who had caught his eye – and heart – despite Anna Neagle's presence in the line. For her, marriage was not 'on' without a settled job. So Bernard took part in one last show to put backbone into his bank balance.

One of the Depression's blank-windowed shops in Soho attracted his attention. 'Take it,' counselled his father. 'There are as many people here in a quarter mile radius as in the whole of Whitstable.'

He did just that. And, on opening day, four and a half thousand green bearded Essex oysters were tricycled out of Soho to London's West End restaurants. But this oyster 'Tour de Londres' soon ceased when he learned that the Criterion was selling his oysters (together with half a pint of Guinness and brown bread and butter) at a welcome profit. There was change enough still from his stage earnings for four tables and sixteen chairs from Whiteley's – at £14 the lot! So in 1929 Wheeler's Oyster Bar was born.

A white-jacketed Bernard Walsh with Ena, his first wife, beside him, dextrously opened oysters from 8 a.m. to midnight, seven days a week. He started as he meant to continue, selecting and sticking to the best. 'Quality fairly priced' was the watchword. Potatoes were taboo. The occasional dissatisfied customer was politely asked to make out his own bill – or pay nothing at all.

Bernard's hospitality to the famous Thursday Club created by Antony Wysard must have been costly. But it set him off on a new tack. They asked for 'something hot' so he cooked them lobster soup laced with champagne on a primus stove. A brilliant Chinese saucier chef Mr Song who had brought culinary joy to the Kit Kat Club and the Café de Paris came 'on the market'. Bernard snapped him up and Wheeler's long list of fish dishes was on the way to fame. Eleven ways of cooking lobster, twenty-five of Dover sole, Sole Germain, Sole du Barry, Sole Colbert, it sounded like a quick scamper through French history.

The oyster bar that could have been 'ringed with a seine-net' was to become a chain of restaurants respected wherever there were seafood devotees. Each one with its own character, for the boy who had spurned school had the intuitive eye of a connoisseur for prints and pictures, china and ceramics.

Success never went to his head. The 'Guv'nor' always kept close contact with his staff – few left him and none ever asked his help in vain. But now he had more time and resources to indulge his great love – racing. From owning a string of horses, among them Luminach and Midsummer Star that so nearly – but never quite – gave him the distinction of leading-in a Classic winner, and from betting, often successfully, though seldom on the 'big ones', he obtained enormous pleasure. And with sponsorship of races for often unappreciated apprentices, he put back into racing as much as he took out.

In a frustrating illness that rendered him immobile, his second wife Brenda, his form books and his television sets (switched to different Channels and courses) were his solace. Indeed it was after he had enjoyed watching the Wheeler's Restaurant Handicap on TV, and hearing Peter O'Sullevan express regret that Bernard Walsh could not be there to present the prizes, that he died. And typical of the man, his Will (safeguarding the family to which he was devoted) decreed that after his funeral, champagne – not tears – should flow.

Let the last word be with C.P. Snow of *The Times*: 'Bernard Walsh was rich in character, vision and hospitality; a man wise and kind whose word was never broken.'

Index of Recipes

Index of Contributors